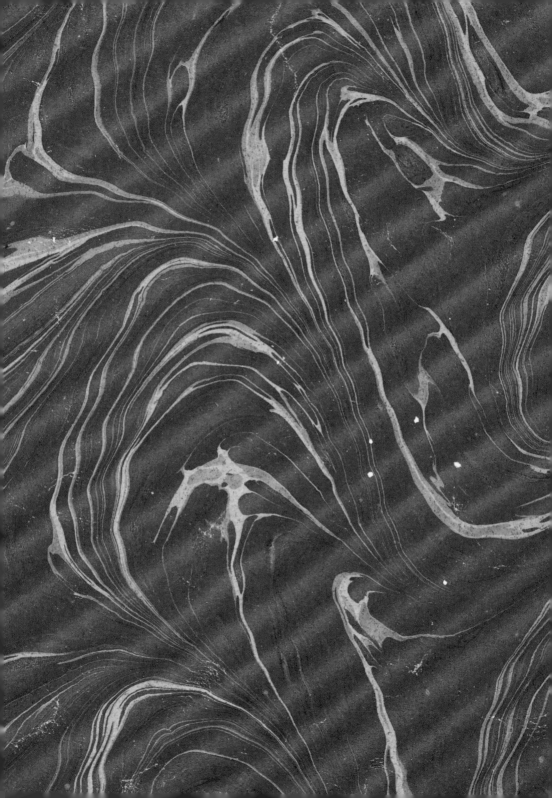

The
World's
Greatest
Letters

A Bundle of Letters

If the band should snap,
the room would fill with voices
flickering like birds

R. A. Johnson, contemporary English writer

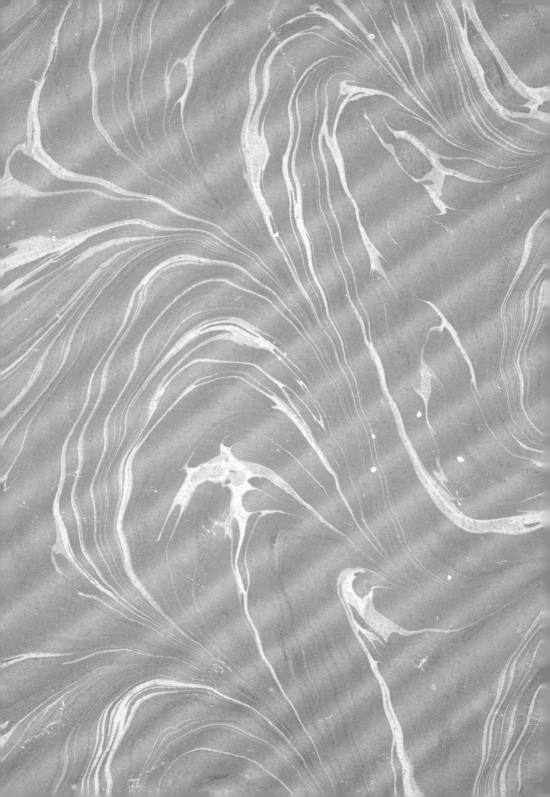

The
World's
Greatest
Letters

From Ancient Greece
to the Twentieth Century

compiled by Michelle Lovric

CHICAGO
REVIEW
PRESS

The World's Greatest Letters

Conception and compilation copyright © 2002 Michelle Lovric
Additional research by Kristina Blagojevitch
and Nicolette Hardee
Editorial assistant: Fiona Johnston
Designed by Michelle Lovric and Lisa Pentreath
Manufactured in China by Imago

Published in the United States and Canada in 2004 by
Chicago Review Press, Incorporated
814 North Franklin Street
Chicago, Illinois 60610
ISBN: 1-55652-549-4

0 9 8 7 6 5 4 3 2 1

The editors gratefully acknowledge the help of
James Spates and Christina Gee.

contents

Write freely, but not hastily; let your Words drop from your Pen, as they would from your Tongue when speaking deliberately on a Subject of which you're Master, and to a Person with whom you're intimate.

The Complete Letter Writer, or Polite English Secretary, 1758

foreword

The excitement of examining primary historical materials, such as manuscript letters, is reserved for a fortunate few scholars. But it is also an intimate and satisfying experience to read an eyewitness account, even if printed in a book, of an important event or relationship by someone who was truly involved in it.

Personalities and motives are nowhere more clearly revealed than in letters. For this reason, as Christopher Morley once observed, letters make the very best anthologies. A collection of letters is the freshest insight into the past, reminding us that what is now history was once real life lived by individuals as full of sensitivities, appetites, passions and prejudices as we are. As Morley so aptly puts it, letters provide 'the mother-of-pearly shimmer inside the oyster of Fact'.

Trawling the world's literature for this selection of the world's greatest letters has proved no small task. The British Library's catalogue alone lists more than fifty thousand volumes of individual correspondence. Moreover, paper being the most perishable and fragile of substances, it is tantalizing to think how many more great letters have perished, never been published, or are still secreted in attics and strong-boxes awaiting discovery.

To find the best and most interesting letters, and to represent all aspects of the epistolary art — intellectual, spiritual and emotional — we concentrated our research on five kinds of correspondence: Love, Family and Friends, Human Creativity, History, Science and Human Endeavour.

Some of our letter writers appear in more than one category. This is not surprising, as some of the world's best correspondents were also among the greatest lovers or were eyewitnesses to the important events of their day.

Space reasons have precluded the inclusion of entire letters in most cases. Abridgement has also been necessary for other reasons: in the days when letters were the only means of communication, they were loaded down with much mundane but essential information. It is sometimes said that the telephone, fax and e-mail have killed off the letter. In fact, new technology has liberated the letter from the need to give shopping lists and urgent news: such things are now handled in quick electronic exchanges that leave no trace and when someone sits down to write a letter these days, it is an occasion; modern letters are possibly the better for it. Future anthologists will find out ...

Exchanges of letters between lovers and familiars are rarely brief. Particularly in the case of love letters, they often run to dozens, or even hundreds of letters, as in the case of Elizabeth Barrett and Robert Browning, whose love affair indeed commenced in writing. It is, consequently, difficult to capture the flavour of a whole romance, or the personality of the writer in just one sample letter. Therefore we have often included excerpts from various letters to better illustrate the nature of the writer and the love affair. The same is often true of long-running friendships transacted by post and in these cases too we have chosen extracts.

Finally, a note on the text. Throughout history, personal letters were often scribbled in haste and contain involuntary errors. Other early letters were written in archaic language that would make them hard to read with pleasure these days. In both cases we have in general instituted standard English spellings and modern English wording. Some mistakes have been left as they were, in order to preserve the personality of the writer and the tone of the letter. Our criterion has been readability: the need to preserve a connection between the writer and the modern-day reader.

Michelle Lovric,
Kristina Blagojevitch and Nicolette Hardee
London, July 2002

Love Letters & Writing About Love

The public will always give up
its dinner to read love letters.

George Jean Nathan (1882—1958)
American editor and critic

Sappho

Sappho (612—580 BC), Greek poetess, dedicated these lines to her lover, Anactoria, seventh century BC.

Some say that the fairest thing upon the dark earth is a host of foot-soldiers, and others again a fleet of ships, but for me it is my beloved.

...

Pliny the Younger

Pliny the Younger (62—113), Roman lawyer and writer, sent these letters to his beloved third wife, Calpurnia, first century AD.

You kindly tell me my absence very sensibly affects you, and that your only consolation is in conversing with my works, which you frequently substitute in my place by your side. How agreeable is it to me to know that you thus wish for my company! And support yourself under the want of it by these consolations! In return, I entertain myself with reading over your letters again and again, and am continually taking them up, as if I had but just then received them; but, alas! they only serve to make me more feelingly regret your absence; for how amiable must *her* conversation be whose letters have so many charms!

I lie awake the greatest part of the night in thinking of you ... my feet carry me of their own accord to your apartment at those hours I used to visit you; but not finding you there, I return with as much sorrow and disappointment as an excluded lover.

...

Héloïse

Héloïse (c. 1100—64), a French nun, wrote a famed series of love letters to the philosopher Peter Abelard, who had been her tutor and whom she secretly married. When the affair was discovered, Héloïse was hidden in a convent, but meanwhile Abelard was attacked and castrated by order of her enraged Uncle Fulbert. Héloïse was forced to become a nun. After these events, around 1120, commenced the long and often very cerebral correspondence between the couple. Héloïse suffered painfully from the loss of their love and physical passion. Abelard, not surprisingly, was more philosophical. The two were reunited in death, eventually buried together in the Père-Lachaise cemetery in Paris. Below are some extracts from Héloïse's letters.

If there is anything that may properly be called happiness here below, I am persuaded it is the union of two persons who love each other with perfect liberty, who are united by a secret inclination, and satisfied with each other's merits. Their hearts are full and leave no vacancy for any other passion; they enjoy perpetual tranquillity because they enjoy content ...

What cannot letters inspire? They have souls; they can speak; they have in them all that force which expresses the transports of the heart; they have all the fire of our passions. They can raise them as much as if the persons themselves were present. They have all the tenderness and the delicacy of speech, and sometimes even a boldness of expression beyond it. Letters were first invented for consoling such solitary wretches as myself! ... Having lost the substantial pleasures of seeing and possessing you, I shall in some measure compensate this loss by the satisfaction I shall find in your writing. There I shall read your most sacred thoughts ...

These pleasures of love which we tasted together were so sweet to me that the memory cannot displease me nor can they be erased from my mind. Whichever way I turn, they present themselves, they thrust themselves upon my gaze with the desires which they awaken; their deceiving images do not spare even my sleep. In the solemnity of the mass, when prayer should be purer than at any other time, the licentious pictures of these pleasures so take this miserable heart that I am more occupied by their baseness than by prayer. I ought to groan for the faults I have committed, and I sigh only after those which I can no more commit.

It is not only that which we have done, it is the hours, it is the places which have witnessed what we have done, which are so deeply graven on my heart with thy image, that I find myself again with thee in the same places, during the same hours, doing the same things: even asleep I find no repose. Sometimes the movements of my body betray the thoughts in my soul, words escape me which I cannot keep back ...

...

Pietro Bembo

Pietro Bembo (1470—1547), Italian poet and scholar, wrote this letter to Lucrezia Borgia (1480—1519) around 1503. Aged 23, Borgia had already been given in marriage three times in order to cement political alliances for her father, Pope Alexander VI. Her third husband was Alfonzo D'Este, Duke of Ferrara. The year he met her, 1502, Bembo was writing *Gli Asolani*, a dialogue on the nature of love, which he later dedicated to Borgia. The couple exchanged poems and compliments in the courtly, idealized style of the era, and Bembo always carried with him a lock of Borgia's golden hair. (Byron stole a single hair from this lock when he examined the letters in a library in Milan many years later.) Borgia invited Bembo to address her in his correspondence as 'f.f.' to conceal her identity (or this may have been some kind of secret code between them). After the death of her father in 1503, Borgia became politically vulnerable, and the correspondence cooled to polite exchanges.

Eight days have passed since I parted from f.f., and already it is as though I had been eight years away from her, although I can avow that not one hour has passed without her memory which has become such a close companion to my thoughts that now more than ever is it the food and sustenance of my soul; and if it should endure like this a few days more, as seems it must, I truly believe it will in every way have assumed the office of my soul, and I shall then live and thrive on the memory of her as do other men upon their souls and I shall have no life but in this single thought ... Often I find myself recalling, and with what ease, certain words spoken to me, some on the balcony with the moon as witness, others at that window I shall always look upon so gladly, with all the many endearing and gracious acts I have seen my gentle lady perform — for all are dancing about my heart with a tenderness so wondrous that they inflame me with a strong desire to beg her to test the quality of my love. For I shall never rest content until I am certain she knows what she is able to enact in me and how great and strong is the fire that her great worth has kindled in my breast.

...

King Henry VIII of England

King Henry VIII of England (1491—1547) wrote a series of secret love letters to Anne Boleyn, who was to become his second queen in 1533. The letters, some of which were written in French, betrayed his frustration at their separations and asserted his desire to terminate his existing marriage to Catherine of Aragon. But five years after they were married, when Anne had still failed to produce the male heir that Henry craved, she was beheaded for adultery, incest and conspiracy to assassinate Henry — accusations that were almost certainly false. She was survived by a daughter who was to become Elizabeth I. The first letter was written some time before July 1527.

But if it pleases you to play the part of a true, loyal mistress and friend, and to give yourself body and heart to me, who will be, and has been, your most loyal servant (if your rigour does not forbid me), I promise you that not only will you deserve the name, but also that I will take you for my only mistress, casting all others, that are in competition with you, out of my thoughts and affection, and serving only you.

Around July 1528, Henry wrote as follows:

Mine own sweetheart, this shall be to advertise you of the great aloneness that I find here since your departing, for I ensure you, methinketh the time longer since your departing now last than I was wont to do a whole fortnight; I think your kindness and my fervence of Love causeth it, for otherwise I would not have thought it possible, that for so little a while it should have grieved me, but now that I am coming toward you, methinketh my pains by half released, and also I am right well comforted, insomuch that my Book maketh substantially for my matter, in writing whereof I have spent above four hours this day, which caused me now to write the shorter letter to you at this time, because of some pain in my head, wishing my self (specially an evening) in my sweetheart's arms, whose pretty ducks* I trust shortly to kiss. Written with the hand of him that was, is, and shall be yours by his will,

H. R.

* a contemporary colloquial term for breasts.

...

King Henri IV of France

King Henri IV of France (1533—1610) wrote a number of amorous letters to his mistress, Gabrielle d'Estrées. The beautiful and charming d'Estrées first met Henri in November 1590. He was twenty years older, and fell for her instantly. To warn off rival suitors, she was married to an elderly aristocrat in 1591, but the marriage was annulled and she became Henri's unofficial consort. (He was already married to Marguerite de Valois.) D'Estrées died giving birth to Henri's third child in April 1599. Poisoning has sometimes been suspected, as Henri was at that point intending to marry her and make their first son his heir. Henri was a hero of both the battlefield and the bedroom. He wrote love letters to many other women, including Henriette d'Entragues and Marie de Médicis, with whom he subsequently went through a form of marriage. Here are two extracts from his letters to Gabrielle d'Estrées.

February 10th, 1593.

I know not what charm you have employed, but I never endured previous absences with so much impatience as I do this. It seems to me that already a century has elapsed since I departed from you. You have no need to urge me to return; I have neither artery nor muscle which does not at every moment bring the thought of seeing you before me, and make me feel distressed at your absence. Believe me, my dear sovereign, never did love do me such violence as it does now.

June 16th, 1593.

I have waited patiently for one whole day without news of you; I have been counting the time and that's what it must be. But a second day — I can see no reason for it, unless my servants have grown lazy or been captured by the enemy, for I dare not put the blame on you, my beautiful angel: I am too confident of your affection — which is certainly due to me, for my love was never greater, nor my desire more urgent; that is why I repeat this refrain in all my letters: come, come, come, my dear love. Honour with your presence the man who, if only he were free, would go a thousand miles to throw himself at your feet and never move from there.

...

John Winthrop

John Winthrop (1606—76), first Governor of the Massachusetts Bay Colony, used biblical imagery to describe his passion for his fiancée (and later third wife), Margaret Tyndal.

And now, my sweet love, let me awhile solace myself in the remembrance of our love, of which this springtime of our acquaintance can put forth as yet no more but the leaves and blossoms, whilst the fruit lies wrapped up in the tender bud of hope; a little more patience will disclose this good fruit, and bring it to some maturity. Let it be our care and labour to preserve these hopeful buds from the beasts of the field, and from frosts and other injuries of the air, lest our fruit fall off ere it be ripe, or lose aught in the beauty and pleasantness of it. Let us pluck up such nettles and thorns as would defraud our plants of their due nourishment; let us prune off superfluous branches; let us not stick at some labour in watering and manuring them: the plenty and goodness of our fruit shall recompense us abundantly. Our trees are planted in a fruitful soil; the ground and pattern of our love is no other but that between Christ and his dear spouse, of whom she speaks as she finds him. 'My well-beloved is mine and I am his.' Love was their banqueting-house, love was their wine, love was their ensign; love was his invitings, love was her faintings; love was his apples, love was her comforts; love was his embracings, love was her refreshing; love made him see her, love made her seek him; love made him wed her, love made her follow him; love made him her saviour, love made her his servant. Love bred our fellowship, let love continue it, and love shall increase it until death dissolve it ...

...

Edmund Waller

Edmund Waller (1606—87), English poet, described with a somewhat ironic ferocity, his anger at being disappointed in love in a letter to Lady Lucy Sidney. Lady Lucy was the sister of Lady Dorothy Sidney, whom Waller courted unsuccessfully after the death of his wife, commemorating her in verse as 'Sacharissa'. Lady Dorothy married Henry, Lord Spencer in July 1639. This letter was written at that time.

... May my Lady Dorothy, if we may yet call her so, suffer as much, and have the like Passion for this young Lord, whom she has preferr'd to the rest of Mankind, as others have had for her; and may this Love, before the Year go about, make her taste of the first Curse impos'd on Womankind, the Pains of becoming a Mother. May her first-born be none of her own Sex, nor so like her, but that he may resemble her Lord as much as her self.

May she that always affected Silence and Retiredness, have the House fill'd with the Noise and Number of her Children, and hereafter of her Grand-Children, and then may she arrive at that great Curse so much declin'd by fair Ladies, Old Age: May she live to be very old, and yet seem young, be told so by her Glass, and have no Aches to inform her of the Truth: And when she shall appear to be mortal, may her Lord not mourn for her, but go Hand in Hand with her to that Place, where we are told there is neither marrying nor giving in Marriage, that being there divorced, we may all have an equal Interest in her again. My Revenge being immortal, I wish all this may also befall their Posterity, to the World's End, and afterwards.

...

Ninon de L'Enclos

Ninon de L'Enclos (1620—1706) was a brilliant French courtesan in the reign of Louis XIV. Her circle of admirers, drawn as much to her intelligence as her beauty, included Molière and La Rochefoucauld. She wrote many letters to Charles, Marquis de Sévigné, son of the celebrated Madame de Sévigné, to guide him in his courtship of a beautiful countess. In this letter she describes the joys of love.

To-day a new sun rises for me; everything lives, everything is animated, everything seems to speak to me of my passion, everything invites me to cherish it. The fire consuming me gives to my heart, to all the faculties of my soul, a resilience, an activity which is diffused through all my affections. Since I loved you, my friends are dearer to me; I love myself more ... the sounds of my lute seem to me more moving, my voices more harmonious.

Shall I tell you what makes love so dangerous? 'Tis the too high idea we are apt to form of it. But to speak the truth, love, considered as a passion, is merely a blind instinct, that we should rate accordingly. It is an appetite, which inclines us to one object, rather than another, without our being able to account for our taste. Considered as a bond of friendship, where reason presides, it is no longer a passion and loses the very name of love. It becomes esteem: which is indeed a very pleasing appetite, but too tranquil; and therefore incapable of rousing you from your present supineness.

If you madly trace the footsteps of our ancient heroes of romance, adopting their extravagant sentiments, you will soon experience, that such false chivalry metamorphoses this charming passion into a melancholy folly; nay, often a tragical one: a perfect frenzy! but divest it of all the borrowed pomp of opinion, and you will then perceive how much it will contribute both to your happiness and pleasure. Be assured that if either reason or knight-errantry should be permitted to form the union of our hearts, love would become a state of apathy and madness.

The only way to avoid these extremes, is to pursue the course I pointed out to you. At present you have no occasion for any thing more than mere amusement, and believe me, you will not meet it except among women of the character I speak of. Your heart wants occupation; and they are framed to supply the void. At least, give my prescription a fair trial, and I will be answerable for the success.

I promised to reason with you, and I think I have kept my word. Farewell ...

...

John Dryden

John Dryden (1631—1700), English poet, critic and playwright, wrote this graceful letter of thanks to his cousin, Honor Dryden, in May 1653 or 1655.

... my pen is stealing into verse every time I kiss your letter. I am sure the poor paper smarts for my Idolatry, which by wearing it continually near my breast will at last be burnt and martyred in those flames of adoration it hath kindled in me. But I forget Madam what rarities your letter came fraught with besides words; You are such a Deity that commands worship by providing the Sacrifice: you are pleased Madame to force me to write by sending me Materials, and compel me to my greatest happiness. Yet though I highly value your Magnificent presents, pardon me if I must tell the world they are but imperfect Emblems of your beauty; For the white and red of waxe and paper are but shadows of that vermilion and snow in your lips and forehead. And the silver of the Inkhorn if it presume to vie

16

whiteness with your purer Skin, must confess it self blacker than the liquor it contains.

...

Marianna Alcoforado

Marianna Alcoforado, a Portuguese nun, wrote to Noël Bouton de Chamilly, Count of St. Leger (later Marquis of Chamilly) in 1668. He had seduced and then abandoned her, after which she described her plight in a series of famously searing letters. The authenticity of these letters has sometimes been questioned, but the emotional truth of the pain described in them remains undeniably authentic. Here are some short extracts.

I gave my life to you as soon as I saw you, and I feel a certain pleasure in sacrificing it to you. A thousand times a day my sighs go out to you, seeking you everywhere ...

I have made it my honour and my religion to love you desperately ... I wish nothing from you which does not come of your free will, and I refuse all tokens of your love ...

Do what you will; my love no longer depends on the way you may treat me. Since you went away ... my only pleasure consists in naming your name a thousand times a day ...

I thank you from the bottom of my heart for the despair you cause me, and I despise the tranquillity in which I lived before knowing you. Farewell, my passion grows with every moment. Ah, how many things I have to say to you!

...

Dorothy Osborne

Dorothy Osborne (1627—95), English woman of letters, pursued a long epistolary courtship with Sir William Temple, writer and diplomat. Political differences between their families and the exceedingly sensitive personalities of the lovers kept them apart for seven years. They were married on Christmas Day 1654. Their marriage was mutually satisfactory and supportive. Temple apparently destroyed his side of the correspondence when Osborne died in 1695. These extracts give a flavour of the cerebral but often anguished nature of their relationship.

c. 1652—54.

We have lived hitherto upon hopes so airy that I have often wondered how they could support the weight of our misfortunes; but passion gives a strength above nature, we see it in mad people; and, not to flatter ourselves, ours is but a refined degree of madness. What can it be else to be lost to all things in the world but that single object that takes up one's fancy, to lose all the quiet and repose of one's life in hunting after it, when there is so little likelihood of ever gaining it, and so many more probable accidents that will infallibly make us miss of it?

But what an age 'tis since we first met, and how great a change it has wrought in both of us; if there had been as great a one in my face, it would be either very handsome or very ugly. For God sake, when we meet, let us design one day to remember old stories in, to ask one another by what degrees our friendship grew to this height 'tis at. In earnest, I am lost sometimes with thinking on't; and though I can never repent the share you have in my heart, I know not whether I gave it you willingly or not at first. No, to speak ingenuously, I think you got an interest there a good while before I thought you had any, and it grew so insensibly, and yet so fast, that all the traverses it has met with since has served rather to discover it to me than at all to hinder it. By this confession you will see I am past all disguise with you, and that you have reason to be satisfied with knowing as much of my heart as I do myself.

March 6th, 1653(?).

Your last letter came like a pardon to one upon the block. I have given over the hopes on't, having received my letters by the other carrier, who uses always to be last. The loss put me hugely out of order, and you would both have pitied me and laughed at me if you could have seen how woodenly I entertained the widow, who came hither the day before, and surprised me very much. Not being able to say anything, I got her to cards, and there with a great deal of patience lost my money to her — or rather I gave it as my ransom. In the midst of our play, in comes my blessed boy with your letter, and, in earnest, I was not able to disguise the joy it gave me, though one was by that is not much your friend, and took notice of a blush that for my life I could not keep back. I put up the letter in my pocket, and made what haste I could to lose the money I had left, that I might take occasion to go fetch some more; but I did not make such a haste back again, I can assure you.

Dorothy tells Temple to preserve himself from the violence of his passions by venting them on her. She asks for his forgiveness, January 7th, 1654.

If you have ever loved me, do not refuse the last request I shall ever make you; 'tis to preserve yourself from the violence of your passion. Vent it all upon me; call me and think me what you please;

make me, if it be possible, more wretched than I am. I'll bear it all without the least murmur. Nay, I deserve it all, for had you never seen me you had certainly been happy. 'Tis my misfortunes only that have the infectious quality as to strike at the same time me and all that's dear to me. I am the most unfortunate woman breathing, but I was never false.

...

Sir Richard Steele

Sir Richard Steele (1672—1729), Irish essayist, dramatist and politician, founder of and contributor to *Tatler* and the *Spectator*, wrote more than 400 letters to Mary Scurlock, his second wife. He was an attentive suitor and husband. Mary sold his playful and charming letters very profitably after his death. They were married soon after these letters were written.

August 14th, 1707.

The Vainest Woman upon Earth never saw in Her Glasse half the attractions which I view in you, your Air, Yr Shape, Your every glance Motion and Gesture have such peculiar Graces that you possesse my whole Soul, and I know no life but in the hopes of your approbation; I know not what to say but that I love you with the Sincerest passion that ever enter'd the Heart of Man. I will make it the businesse of my Life to find out means of Convincing You that I prefer you to All that's pleasing upon earth.

August 1707.

I Lay down last night with your Image in my thoughts, and have awak'd this morning in the same contemplation. The pleasing Transport with which I'me delighted, has a sweetnesse in it attended with a Train of Ten thousand soft desires, anxieties, and cares; The day arises on my hopes with new Brightnesse; Youth Beauty and Innocence are the charming objects that Steal me from myself, and give me Joys above the reach of Ambition pride or Glory. Beleive me, Fair One, to throw myself at your Feet is giving myself the highest blisse I know on Earth. Oh hasten Ye Minutes! bring on the happy Morning wherein to be ever her's will make me look down on Thrones!

August 30th, 1707.

Dear Lovely Mrs. Scurlock, I have been in very good company, where your health, under the character of *the woman I loved best*, has been often drunk; so that I may say that I am dead drunk for your sake, which is more than *I die for you*.

September 1st, 1707.

It is the hardest thing in the world to be in love, and yet attend business. As for me, all who speak to me find out, and I must lock myself up, or other people will do it for me.

A gentleman asked me this morning, 'What news from Lisbon?' and I answered, 'She is exquisitely handsome.' Another desired to know 'when I had last been at Hampton Court?' I replied, 'It will be on Tuesday come se'nnight.' Pr'ythee allow me at least to kiss your hand before that day, that my mind may be in some composure. O Love!

A thousand torments dwell about thee,
Yet who could live, to live without thee?

Methinks I could write a volume to you; but all the language on earth would fail in saying how much, and with what disinterested passion,

I am ever yours.

...

Lady Mary Pierrepont

Lady Mary Pierrepont (1689—1762), English woman of letters, wrote this letter to her future husband, Edward Wortley Montagu, with whom she eloped in August 1712. The courtship was tortured and the marriage proved unsatisfying for the spirited Lady Mary, who became one of the great British eccentrics, and corresponded with many of the eminent literary figures of her time, including Alexander Pope.

The following letter was written on the eve of her elopement, August 15th, 1712.

I tremble for what we are doing. Are you sure you will love me forever? Shall we never repent? I fear, and I hope. I foresee all that will happen on this occasion. I shall incense my family to the highest degree. The generality of the world will blame my conduct, and the relations and friends of —— will invent a thousand stories of me, yet — 'tis possible you may recompense everything to me.

October 22nd, 1712.

I don't know whether you will presently find out that this seeming impertinent account is the tenderest expressions of my love to you, but it furnishes my imagination with agreeable pictures of our future life, and I flatter myself with the hope of one day enjoying with you the same satisfactions, and that after as many years together I may see you retain the same fondness for me as I shall certainly mine for you; and the noise of a nursery may have more charms for us than the music of an opera.

Years later, Lady Mary separated from her husband and fell in love with a young Italian writer, Francesco Algarotti. This letter, dated August 1736, shows how freely she could express herself.

I no longer know how to write to you. My feelings are too ardent; I could not possibly explain them or hide them. One would have to be affected by an enthusiasm similar to mine to endure my letters. I see all its folly without being able to correct myself. The very idea of seeing you again gave me a shock while I read your letter, which almost made me swoon. What has become of that philosophical indifference that made the glory and the tranquillity of my former days? I have lost it never to find it again, and if that passion is healed I foresee nothing except mortal ennui. — Forgive the absurdity that you have brought into being, and come to see me.

...

Esther Vanhomrigh

Esther ('Vanessa') Vanhomrigh (1690—1723) was one of several women seduced by the wit and charm of the Irish writer Jonathan Swift. She was the daughter of his London landlady, and their secret affair lasted many years, throughout which he was two-timing her with another Esther — this time Esther Johnston, whom he called 'Stella', and to whom he addressed a kind of letter-journal of his life. Under duress it appears that the caddish Swift eventually married 'Stella'. Meanwhile, the spurned 'Vanessa', when attempting to intervene, was met with a shockingly cold reaction from Swift, and pined to death. In their correspondence Swift had taken the name 'Cadenus', which his wretched lover appropriately shortened to 'Cad' in some of her imploring letters. This letter was written between 1719 and 1720.

I believe you thought I only rallied when I told you the other night I would pester you with letters. Did not I know you very well, I should think you knew but little of the world, to imagine that a woman would not keep her word whenever she promised anything that was malicious. Had you not better a thousand times throw away one hour, at some time or other of the day, than to be interrupted in your business at this rate? For I know 'tis as impossible for you to burn my letters without reading them, as tis for me to avoid reproving you when you behave yourself so wrong. Once more I advise you, if you have any regard for your quiet, to alter your behaviour quickly, for I do assure you I have too much spirit to sit down contented with this treatment. Now, because I love frankness extremely, I here tell you that I have determined to try all manner of human arts to reclaim you, and if all those fail I am resolved to have recourse to the black one, which [it] is said, never does. Now see what inconvenience you will bring both me and yourself into. Pray think calmly of it. Is it not much better to come of yourself than to be brought by force, and that, perhaps, at a time when you have the most agreeable engagement in the world? For when I undertake anything, I don't love to do it by halves. But there is one thing falls out very luckily for you, which is, that of all the passions revenge hurries me least, so that you have it yet in your power to turn all this fury into good humour, and depend upon it, and more, I assure you. Come at what time you please, you can never fail of being very well received.

...

Voltaire

Voltaire (François-Marie Arouet) (1694—1778), French writer and philosopher, fell in love with Olympe Dunoyer when he was nineteen and working in The Hague as attaché to the French ambassador. The audacious Dunoyer dressed in men's clothes for their secret meetings. The match was opposed on all sides. Voltaire was eventually imprisoned by the ambassador, but he escaped by climbing out of the window, and fled with Dunoyer (nicknamed 'Pimpette') to Scheveningen, en route to Paris. The lovers were intercepted, and the great romance came to nothing. This letter is dated 1713.

I am a prisoner here in the name of the King; they can take my life, but not the love that I feel for you. Yes, my adorable mistress, tonight I shall see you, and if I had to put my head on the block to do it. For Heaven's sake, do not speak to me in such disastrous terms as you write, you must live and be cautious; beware of madame your mother as of your worst enemy. What do I say? Beware of everybody, trust no one; keep yourself in readiness, as soon as the moon is visible; I shall leave the hotel incognito, take a carriage or a chaise, we shall drive like the wind to Scheveningen; I shall take paper and ink with me; we shall write our letters.

If you love me, reassure yourself, and call all your strength and presence of mind to your aid; do not let mother notice anything, try to have your picture, and be assured that the menace of the greatest tortures will not prevent me to serve you.

No, nothing has the power to part me from you; our love is based upon virtue, and will last as long as our lives. Adieu, there is nothing that I will not brave for your sake; you deserve much more than that. Adieu, my dear heart!

Later Voltaire became entangled with Madame Marie Louise Denis, his niece. They became lovers on the death of her husband in 1744, though the romance had long been latent. Voltaire eventually gave up the faithless, corrupt Denis, who hurt and deceived him several times. Many of their playful and erotic letters were written in Italian, including this one, dated December 1745.

You have written me a ravishing letter, which I have kissed. I am not surprised that you write so well in Italian. It is very right and proper that you should be expert in the language of love. Good heavens! I cannot believe you when you tell me that you have no lover. How do you manage? Are so many charms really buried in disuse? You, not going to bed with anyone? Oh my dear one, you insult your god. You tell me that my letter gave pleasure even to your senses. Mine are like yours, I could not read the delicious words you wrote me without feeling inflamed to the depths of my being. I paid your letter the tribute I should have liked to pay to the whole of your person. The pleasures of the senses pass and flee in the twinkle of an eye, but the affection that binds us, the mutual confidence, the pleasures of the heart, the sensual joys of the soul, are not destroyed and do not perish thus. I will love you until death.

March 7th, 1750.

I feel as though I were in a strange country. My real home is where you are. All else is foreign to me. You are my whole family, my Court, my Versailles, my Parnassus, and the sole hope of my heart.

...

Benjamin Franklin

Benjamin Franklin (1706—90), American statesman, diplomat and philosopher, fell in love with Madame d'Hardancourt Brillon when he was posted to Paris. Despite his unpaternal inclinations, the French society woman often referred to him affectionately as 'my dear Papa', as she might well do, being almost 40 years his junior. Interestingly, one of Franklin's most famous letters, to a young male friend, recommended the taking of old rather than young women as mistresses, partly because 'in the Dark all Cats are grey, the pleasure of Corporal Enjoyment with an old Woman is at least equal and frequently superior; every Knack by Practice capable by improvement'. Moreover, Franklin concluded, older mistresses 'are so grateful!!!' This letter to Madame d'Hardancourt Brillon is dated November 10th, 1779.

. What a difference, my dear friend, between you and me! You find innumerable faults in me, whereas I see only one fault in you (but perhaps it is the fault of my glasses). I mean this kind of avarice which leads you to seek a monopoly on all my affections, and not to allow me any for the agreeable ladies of your country. Do you imagine that it is impossible for my affection (or my tenderness) to be divided without being diminished? You deceive yourself, and you forget the playful manner with which you stopped me. You renounce and totally exclude all that might be of the flesh in our affection, allowing me only some kisses, civil and honest, such as you might grant your little cousins. What am I receiving that is so special as to prevent me from giving the same to others, without taking from what belongs to you?

...

William Pitt the Elder

William Pitt the Elder (1708—78), Earl of Chatham and English statesman, fell in love with Lady Hester Grenville when he was 46. They were married on November 16th, 1754 and enjoyed lifelong mutual satisfaction. These extracts give a flavour of the charm of their correspondence.

October 12th, 1754.

Then I may have the honour and consolation to address a few words to my Lady Hester Grenville, a dear object to which my soul directs every thought; and in which I had so lately the happiness to fix my every look with delight, and to pour out my Heart at her feet, in effusions of the most respectful Passion, sweeten'd and endeared to me by the happy sense of Infinite and most touching Obligations. This was my exalted felicity a few days ago.

October 16th, 1754.

I find no paper large enough for a Heart that you permit to be yours.

October 19th, 1754.

What guardian angel of mine can have so blinded you and pour'd into your noble Heart a tender delusion ... as to draw from you so sweet an excess of everything, that can exalt and bless me above the lot of mortals?

October 21st, 1754.

T'was infinite Goodness, t'was Tenderness and Delicacy itself, t'was you my sweetest Life.

...

Samuel Johnson

Samuel Johnson (1709—84), English writer and critic, appointed the English woman of letters Hester Thrale as his muse. She lost his esteem when she married the Italian violinist Gabriele Piozzi in 1784. This letter was written at that time.

Madam,

If I interpret your letter right, you are ignominiously married; if it is yet undone, let us at once more talk together. If you have abandoned your children and your religion, God forgive your wickedness; if you have forfeited your fame and your country, may your folly do no further mischief.

If the last act is yet to do, I, who have loved you, esteemed you, reverenced you, and served you, I who long thought you the first of womankind, entreat that, before your fate is irrevocable, I may once more see you.

I was, I once was,

Madam, most truly yours,

    Sam: Johnson

...

Jean-Jacques Rousseau

Jean-Jacques Rousseau (1712—78), French philosopher and writer, fell in love with Countess Sophie d'Houdetot. Rousseau had fathered five children with his long-term mistress and Sophie was involved with another man, but they did not appear to be able to resist each other, as demonstrated in this letter dated June 1757.

Come, Sophie, that I may torture your unjust heart in order that I, on my side, may be merciless towards you. Why should I spare you, whilst you rob me of reason, of honour, and life? Why should I allow your days to pass in peace, you, who make mine unbearable! — Ah, much less cruel would you have been, if you had driven a dagger into my heart, instead of the fateful weapon, which kills me! Look what I was and what I am now; look to what a degree you have abased me. When you deigned to be mine, I was more than a man; since you have driven me from you, I am the least of mortals. I have lost all reason, all understanding, and all courage; in a word, you have taken everything from me! How could you determine to destroy your own handiwork? How can you dare to consider him as unworthy of esteem, whom you honoured once with your graciousness? Ah, Sophie, I beseech you, do not be ashamed of a friend, whom you once favoured. For your own honour I demand you to render me an account of myself. Am I not your property? Have you not taken possession of me? That you cannot deny, and as I belong to you in spite of myself and of yourself, so let me at least deserve to be yours. Think of those times of happiness, which, to my torture, I shall never forget. That invisible flame from which I received a second, more precious life, rendered to my soul and my senses the whole force of youth. The glow of my feelings raised me to you. How often was not your heart, filled with love for another, touched by the passion of mine. How often did you not say to me in the grove by the waterfall, 'You are the most tender lover, that I can imagine; no, never did a man love like you!' What a triumph for me, such a confession from your lips! Yes, it was real! it was worthy of the passion from which I demanded so ardently, that it should make you receptive, and with which I wished to awake in you a compassion that you now regret so bitterly ...

O Sophie, after all the sweet moments the thought of an eternal renunciation is terrible for him, whom it saddens deeply that he cannot identify himself with you. What! your touching eyes will never droop again before my glances with that sweet shame, which so intoxicated me with sensuous desire? I am never more to feel that heavenly shudder, that maddening, devouring fire, which quicker than lightning ... oh, inexpressible moment! What heart, what god could have experienced you and resisted?

...

Julie de Lespinasse

Julie de Lespinasse (1732—76), French woman of letters, probably died of her hopeless love for Comte Hippolyte de Guibert. They became lovers in 1774, but he abandoned her, and after he married in 1775 she became addicted to opium and pined away. The 180 lyrical love letters that she wrote were first published in 1809, and are classics of French literature. Here are some short extracts.

1773.

All these last days you have tortured my soul. I saw you this morning; I forgot everything, and it seemed to me I was not doing enough for you in loving you with my whole soul, and being ready to live and die for you.

1774.

You have alternately entranced and torn my soul.

November 13th, 1774.

You are the pleasure, the last gratification of the vanity of nearly every woman. By what fatality did you recall me to life, only to make me die of trouble and grief? My love, I do not complain of you, but it afflicts me that you do not put any value on my peace of mind; this thought alternately preys and tears me. How can one have an instant's peace with a man whose behaviour is as reckless as his driving, who cares nothing for dangers, who never foresees anything, who is incapable of little cares, of any exactitude, who never puts through a project, in a word a man attracted by everything but whom nothing can stop or fix? Oh, my God, my God, it is in your wrath, in the excess of your vengeance, you have condemned me to love, to adore one that must become the torment and the despair of my soul. Yes, my love, what you term your faults may kill me, but they will never make me cold towards you. If my will, my reason, my reflection were of any use to me, should I love you? Alas, in how short a time have I been thrust into, cast down the abyss of unhappiness! I still shudder.

February 10th, 1775.

Midnight strikes, and I, my love, am struck by a memory that freezes my blood. It was on the tenth of February last year that I was intoxicated with a poison the effects of which I still feel. In this moment it alters the circulation of my blood which it carries with increased violence to my heart, filling it with agonizing regrets. Alas, by what fatality must the sentiment of the liveliest pleasure be joined to the most overwhelming unhappiness! What a frightful union! Should I not say to myself when I recall that moment of mingled horror and pleasure — I saw a young man, with a glance full of life and sensibility, come towards me, his face expressed sweetness and tenderness, his soul seemed animated by passion. At this sight I was filled with fright mingled with pleasure — I dared to raise my eyes, to fix my glance on him, I advanced, my senses, my soul, were frozen, I saw him advance, sorrow, in a mourning habit, held his arm, he stopped me, tried to hold me off, yet, by a fatal attraction I was drawn on. Speaking from the depth of my distress, I asked, 'Who art thou, who fillest my soul with alarm and tenderness, terror and charm! What news dost thou bring me?' 'Unfortunate one,' he replied with a sombre air and a sad accent, 'I am your Destiny. He who animated your life is now struck with Death.' Yes, my love, I heard these fatal words — they are engraved on my heart, which still shudders, which loves you! In pity let me see you tomorrow; I am full of sadness and trouble ... I perish with regret; my eyes and my heart are full of tears. Farewell, my love. I ought not to love you.

...

Johann Wolfgang von Goethe

Johann Wolfgang von Goethe (1749—1832), German poet and dramatist, fell in love with Charlotte Buff, who was engaged to and eventually married his friend Kestner. They continued to correspond passionately, even after her marriage. Goethe's agony was played out in his novel *The Sorrows of Young Werther*, the story of a pure and hopeless passion which made him famous all over Europe. Goethe later became involved with Charlotte von Stein. He was 26 and already precociously famous when he met Frau von Stein, a married woman of 33, who had already borne seven children (to whom Goethe referred as the 'Meerkatzen'). It is possible that the love affair, though intense, was never consummated. The relationship foundered when Goethe took a young mistress, Christiane Vulpius, in 1788. Goethe had several children with Vulpius, but did not marry her until 1806, only to fall in love with Minna Herzlieb immediately afterwards. Goethe's amorous exploits continued until he was 74. This letter, to Charlotte von Stein, is dated December 23rd, 1786.

Only let me thank you for your letter! Let me forget for a moment the painful part of its contents. My love! my love! Let me beg from you on my knees, imploringly, make my return to you easier, that I may not remain banished in the wide world.

Pardon me generously for my sins towards you, and raise me up. Tell me oft and at length, how you live, that you are well, that you love me. In my next letter I will let you know my travel-itinerary, what I had proposed doing, and may Heaven let it prosper. Only I beg of you; do not regard me as separated from you, nothing in the world can replace to me, what I should lose both in you and in my circumstances there. May I bring back the strength to suffer more manfully every contrariety.

...

Honoré-Gabriel Riquetti

Honoré-Gabriel Riquetti (1749—91), Comte de Mirabeau, French revolutionary leader, fell in love with Sophia Ruffey, wife of the Marquis de Monnier, some time in 1777. They eloped and he was later imprisoned, during which time she bore a child who sadly succumbed to convulsions. The lovers never met again. While in prison, Mirabeau wrote an erotic novel, which was smuggled out to his mistress in instalments, along with a series of impassioned love letters. Here are some extracts.

Undated, 1777—78.

I love you because I live. Love is the breath of my life. To think of ceasing to adore you seems to me as absurd as to think of continuing to live without a heart to pump the blood through my veins or without lungs wherewith to breathe. My Sophie, I can take no more merit to myself for loving you, than the streams for flowing into the sea or the fire for burning: it is my nature, the very essence of my life ...

I have told you again and again, that the perfume of your breath as you press your lips to mine stirs me a thousand times more deeply than any emotions, however poignant, that I have ever felt in the arms of other women. It is a triumph that you may not fully appreciate, my dearest, but it consoles me when I think of how I have laid my homage at the feet of so many other beautiful women, by showing me the difference between the desires of nature and those of love; proving to me, consequently, that I have never loved any but you ...

August 27th, 1777.

I bled a great deal from the nose last night, my darling, and that woke me from a lovely dream. I was with you at P... We were alone; I was moistening with my lips the pupils of your eyes, which you were about to close in death; upon them lay the gentle burden of my kisses. With my love I enveloped you; heart called to heart; heart answered to heart: our breaths mingled and formed a lovely, voluptuous murmur; sighs took the place of words, which we seemed no longer able to utter; I, at that moment, passed away: your spirit was about to follow mine, when ... Alas! the illusion fled like an airy mist ... Oh my dear! these vivid dreams show me the object of my desires; but I cannot enjoy ... the pleasure they afford fades away so soon, so soon! Far from assuaging my thirst they only serve to increase it a hundredfold.

...

Wolfgang Amadeus Mozart

Wolfgang Amadeus Mozart (1756—91), Austrian composer, maintained a bawdy, affectionate correspondence with his wife, Constanze, a pianist and singer. They married in 1782, against the wishes of his dominating father, and with subsequent financial problems. Mozart's letters are, nevertheless, generally full of fun. This letter was written on April 16th, 1789.

Darling wife, I have a number of requests to make to you: —
1st. I beg you will not be melancholy.
2nd. That you will take care of yourself, and not expose yourself to the spring breezes.
3rd. That you will not go out to walk alone — indeed, it would be better not to walk at all.
4th. That you will feel entirely assured of my love.

October 17th, 1790.

While I was writing the last page, tear after tear fell on the paper. But I must cheer up — catch! — An astonishing number of kisses are flying about — The deuce! — I see a whole crowd of them! Ha! Ha! ... I have just caught three — They are delicious! — You can still answer this letter, but you must address your reply to Linz, Poste Restante — That is the safest course ... Adieu — Dearest, most beloved little wife — Take care of your health — and don't think of walking into town. Do write and tell me how you like our new quarters — Adieu. I kiss you millions of times.

29

Horatio Nelson

Horatio Nelson (1758—1805), English naval officer, found the love of his life in Lady Emma Hamilton. Emma was born to humble parents in 1761 and grew up in Wales. She came successively under the 'protection' of Sir Harry Fetherstonehaugh and then Charles Greville, whom she loved passionately. He rather callously handed her on to his uncle, Sir William Hamilton, whom she married in 1791, despite the vast differences in their age, social rank and education. She was living with Sir William in Naples when she first met Nelson, a celebrated hero for his naval victories. From 1798, the two enjoyed a wildly indiscreet affair and Emma bore his daughter, Horatia. During that period, Nelson wrote to her using the name 'John Thomson', a crew-member on his own boat. She was 'Mrs Thomson', a member of Lady Hamilton's household. 'Mr Thomson' wrote anxious letters about his wife's impending confinement and with great joy on the birth of the child. Meanwhile, respectful official letters passed between Nelson and Emma, in their public roles. The tolerant Sir William remained deeply fond of Nelson, and even shared a home with the couple for some time. Nelson was killed at the Battle of Trafalgar in 1805. Emma died in poverty in Calais in 1815. Below are some extracts from his letters to her.

January 29th, 1800.

Separated from all I hold dear in this world what is the use of living if indeed such an existance can be called so, nothing could alleviate such a Separation but the call of our Country but loitering time away with nonsense is too much, no Separation no time my only beloved Emma can alter my love and affection for You, it is founded on the truest principles of honor, and it only remains for us to regret which I do with the bitterest anguish that there are any obstacles to our being united in the closest ties of this Worlds rigid rules, as We are in those of real love. Continue only to love Your faithful Nelson as he loves his Emma. You are my guide I submit to You, let me find all My fond heart hopes and wishes with the risk of my life I have been faithful to my word never to partake of any amusement or to sleep on Shore. Thursday Janry 30th We have been Six days from Leghorn and no prospect of our making a passage to Palermo, to me it is worse than death. I can neither Eat or Sleep for thinking of You my dearest love, I never touch even pudding …

Last Night I did nothing but dream of You altho' I woke 20 times in the Night. In one of my dreams I thought I was at a large Table You was not present, Sitting between a Princess who I detest and another. They both tried to Seduce Me and the first wanted to take those liberties with Me which no Woman in this World but Yourself ever did. The consequence was I knocked her down and in the moment of bustle You came in and taking Me in Your embrace wispered I love nothing but You My Nelson. I kissed You fervently And we enjoy'd the height of love. Ah Emma I pour out my Soul to You.

February 17th, 1801, expressing his fears that the Prince Regent would seduce her:

I am so agitated that I can write nothing. I knew it would be so, and you can't help it. Why did you not tell Sir William? Your character will be gone. Good God! he will be next you, and telling you soft things. If he does, tell it out at table, and turn him out of the house. Do not sit long. If you sing a song, I know you cannot help it, do not let him sit next you, but at dinner he will hob glasses with you. I cannot write to Sir Wm, but he ought to go to the Prince and not suffer your character to be ruined by him. O, God, that I was dead! But I do not, my dearest Emma, blame you, nor do I fear your inconstancy. I tremble, and God knows how I write. Can nothing be thought of? I am gone almost mad, but you cannot help it. It will be in all the newspapers with hints. Recollect what the villain said to Mr. Nisbet, *how you hit his fancy*. I am mad, almost dead, but ever for ever yours to the last moment, your, only your, &c.

I could not write another line if I was to be made King. If I was in town nothing should make me dine with you that damned day, but, my dear Emma, I do not blame you, only remember your poor miserable friend, that you must be singing and appear gay. I shall that day have no one to dinner; it shall be a fast day to me. He will put his foot near you. I pity you from my soul, as I feel confident you wish him in hell. Have plenty of people and do not say a word you can help to him. He wishes, I dare say, to have you alone. Don't let him touch, nor yet sit next you; if he comes, get up. God strike him blind if he looks at you — this is high treason, and you may get me hanged by revealing it. Oh, God! that I were. I have read your letter, your resolution never to go where the fellow is, but you must have him at home. Oh, God! but you cannot, I suppose, help it, and you cannot turn him out of your own house. He will stay and sup and sit up till 4 in the morning, and the fewer that stay the better. Oh, God, why do I live? But I do not blame you; it is my misfortune. I feel nobody uses me ill. I am only fit to be second, or third, or 4, or to black shoes. I want no better part than I have. I see your determination to be on your guard, and am as fixed as fate. If you'll believe me, don't scold me; I am more dead than alive, to the last breath yours. If you cannot get rid of this I hope you will tell Sir William never to bring the fellow again.

February 27th, 1801.

Parting from such a friend is literally tearing one's own flesh; but the remembrance will keep up our spirits till we meet. My affection is, if possible, stronger than ever for you, and I trust it will keep increasing as long as we both live. I have seen Mrs. Thomson's friend, who is delighted at my having seen his dear child. I am sure he will be very fond of it. I arrived here before noon, and have had my hands full of business. Tomorrow we embark troops. I will write you a long letter tonight, and send it under cover to Troubridge; therefore you will have it on Sunday. For ever, aye for ever, believe me, &c.

March 1801.

Fancy what would happen, and will happen, when we meet. I can say no more; flattering fancy wafts me to your dear, dear arms.

...

Mary Wollstonecraft

Mary Wollstonecraft (1759—97), Anglo-Irish feminist and writer, wrote this coy and loving letter to William Godwin on October 4th, 1796. She was recovering from a suicidal depression following her previous passion for Gilbert Imlay, the father of her daughter, Fanny, who had abandoned her. Her imploring letters to Imlay make heart-rending reading. She married Godwin on March 29th, 1797. She died giving birth to Mary Godwin, who married the poet Shelley and was the author of *Frankenstein*.

So I must write a line to sweeten your dinner — No; to give you a little salt for your mutton, rather: though your not partaking of a morsel, Mary was bring me up, of this dinner, as you were going out, prevented me from relishing it —

I should have liked to have dined with you to day, after finishing your essay — that my eyes, and lips, I do not exactly mean my voice, might have told you that they had raised you in my *esteem*. What a cold word! I would say love, if you will promise not to dispute about its propriety, when I want to express an increasing affection, founded on a more intimate acquaintance with your heart and understanding.

I shall cork up all my kindness — yet the fine volatile essence may fly off in my walk — you know not how much tenderness for you may escape in a voluptuous sigh, should the air, as is often the case, give a pleasurable movement to the sensations, that have been clustering round my heart, as I read this morning — reminding myself, every now and then, that the writer *loved me*. Voluptuous is often expressive of a meaning I do not now intend to give. I would describe one of those moments, when the senses are exactly tuned by the rising tenderness of the heart, and according reason entices you to live in the present moment, regardless of the past or future — It is not rapture. — It is a sublime tranquillity. I have felt it in your arms — Hush! Let not the light see, I was going to say hear it

— These confessions should only be uttered — you know where, when the curtains are up — and all the world shut out ...

Ah me! What shall I do to day, I anticipate the unpleasing task of repressing kindness — and I am overflowing with the kindest sympathy — I wish I may find you at home when I carry this letter to drop it in the box, — that I may drop a kiss with it into your heart, to be embalmed, till we meet ... closer [crossed out] — Don't read the last word — I charge you!

...

Benjamin Constant de Rebecque

Benjamin Constant de Rebecque (1767—1830), French statesman and novelist, sent this love letter, one of many, to Juliette Récamier, in January 1815. He nursed a hopeless passion for the tantalizing, beautiful and married Madame Récamier, who specialized in enslaving the great men of her age. During Récamier's delicate romance with Constant, she kept him perpetually suspended between mad hope and suicidal despair. The crazed Constant at one point seriously contemplated conjuring up the devil in order to sell his soul in exchange for Récamier's body. His infatuation passed as suddenly as it arose, but during his year of the Récamier 'treatment', Constant wrote some 60 passionate letters to her.

My love is a constant sensation which nothing suspends, which nothing interrupts, which is alternatively absolute devotion which has its sweetness, and an agony so fearful, that if you were to prolong it twice twenty-four hours, you would kill me. Have you not seen yesterday again your power? Do you not feel that every time I speak to you of anything else than my feeling for you, it is a sacrifice that I make. But what sacrifice would I not make to enable me to see you and to hear you! If you knew what enchantment I feel when you speak rather more freely than usual, with a little openness and confidence! how every one of your words goes down into my heart, how my soul fills itself with you! how a repose, a momentary happiness, replace the agitation which devours me elsewhere! Oh, if you loved me as I love you, what happiness would we not enjoy! What certainty would we not have the one from the other in life! If, in awaking, you were to think with pleasure of this feeling which surrounds you, which embraces from the smallest details up to the greatest interests of your existence, which associates itself to every one of your thoughts; which, if you would permit it, would not leave a single one of your emotions, not one of the needs of your heart without reply; of this feeling so exempt of all egoism, which finds in devoting itself the happiness which others seek in self-love and in success; which is a stranger to all other calculations; for which neither glory nor power, nor fortune, nor amusement exist in so far as they are not means to come to you and to serve you or please you ...

...

Napoleon Bonaparte

Napoleon Bonaparte (1769—1821), French ruler, loved the wayward Josephine Beauharnais with a wild and undisciplined passion which contrasted sharply with his precision on the battlefield. Josephine never responded satisfactorily to his urgent desires for her letters or her presence. She was a widow six years his senior when they met. He married her on March 9th, 1796, and she was crowned Empress in 1804, but Napoleon divorced her five years later as she was unable to produce an heir. They continued to write affectionately to each other. The extracts below give a flavour of Napoleon's correspondence at the height of his passion for Josephine.

April 4th, 1796.

By what art have you become able to captivate all my faculties, to concentrate in yourself my moral existence? It is a magic, my sweet love, which will end only with me. To live for Josephine, that is the history of my life. I am trying to reach you, I am dying to be near you ... Time was when I prided myself on my courage, and sometimes when considering the evil which men might be able to do me, the fate which might have in store for me, I fixed my eyes steadfastly on the most unheard-of misfortunes without frowning, without being surprised; but today the idea that my Josephine might be unwell, the idea that she might be ill, and, above all, the cruel, the fatal thought that she might love me less, withers my soul, stops my blood, makes me sad, cast down, and leaves me not even the courage of fury and despair. I often used to say to myself that men could have no power over him who dies without regrets. But today to die without being loved by you, to die without that certainty is the torment of hell, is the lifelike and striking image of absolute annihilation. I feel as if I were being stifled. My only companion, you whom fate has decreed to make with me the painful journey of life, the day when I shall no longer possess your heart will be that when parched Nature will be to me without warmth and without vegetation ... Love me as your eyes — but that is not enough: as yourself, more than yourself; as your thoughts, your mind, your sight, your all. Sweet beloved, forgive me. I am worn out. Nature is weak for him who feels keenly, for him whom you love!

June 16th, 1796.

Your portrait and your letters are ever before my eyes. I am nothing without you. I scarcely imagine how I have existed without knowing you. Ah! Josephine if you had known my heart would you have waited from 19th May to 5th June before starting? Would you have listened to false friends who wished, perhaps, to keep you away from me? I openly admit I hate every one who is near you. I expected you to have set out on 25th May and to have arrived at Milan on 4th June.

Josephine, if you love me, if you believe that everything depends on your keeping in good health, take care of yourself. I dare not tell you not to undertake a journey of such length and in the hot weather. At least if you are well enough to make the journey come by short stages. Write to me at every sleeping-place and send me your letters ahead.

All my thoughts are concentrated in your boudoir, in your bed, on your heart. Your illness that is what occupies my mind night and day. Without appetite, without sleep, without care for my friendships, for glory, for fatherland, you, you and the rest of the world exist no more for me than if it were annihilated. I prize honour since you prize it. I prize victory since that gives you pleasure, without which I should have left all to throw myself at your feet ...

In your letter, my darling, be careful to tell me that you are convinced that I love you beyond all imagining, that you are persuaded that every moment of my life is consecrated to you, that never an hour passes without my thinking of you, that never has the thought of thinking of another woman entered my head, that to my eyes they are lacking in grace, beauty and wit, that you, you only, such as I see you, such as you are, could please me and absorb all the faculties of my mind; that you have influenced it all over, that my heart has no recesses which you do not see, no thoughts which are not subject to you; that my strength, my prowess, my spirit are all yours, that my soul is in your body, and that the day when you shall change or when you shall cease to live, will be my death-day; that nature, the earth are beautiful to my eyes only because you dwell therein. If you do not believe all that, if your mind is not convinced, penetrated by it, you distress me, you love me not. There is a magnetic fluid between people who love one another. You know quite well that I could not bear to let you have a lover, still less to offer you one. To tear out his heart and to see him would be the same thing for me ...

Do you remember the dream in which I was your shoes, your dress, and I made you enter deep into my heart. Why did not Nature arrange matters thus? There are many things that want doing.

William Wordsworth

William Wordsworth (1770—1850), English poet, married Mary Hutchinson in 1802. These extracts from their letters show how even their mature love always retained the freshness of its passion and affection. They had been childhood sweethearts and the strong relationship survived his fathering a daughter with a Frenchwoman, Annette Vallon.

August 11th, 1810.

Every day every hour every moment makes me feel more deeply how blessed we are in each other, how purely how faithfully how ardently, and how tenderly we love each other; I put this last word last because, though I am persuaded that a deep affection is not uncommon in married life, yet I am confident that a lively, gushing, thought-employing, spirit-stirring, passion of love, is very rare even among good people. I will say more upon this when we meet, grounded upon recent observation of the condition of others. We have been parted my sweet Mary too long, but we have not been parted in vain, for wherever I go I am admonished how blessed, and almost peculiar a lot mine is.

May 7th, 1812.

I love thee so deeply and tenderly and constantly, and with such perfect satisfaction delight & happiness to my soul, that I scarcely can bring my pen to write of any thing else. — How blest was I to hear of those sweet thoughts of me which had flowed along thy dreams; sleeping & waking my Love let me be with thee as thou art with me!

May 13th, 1812.

My sweet Love how I long to see thee; think of me, wish for me, pray for me, pronounce my name when thou art alone, and upon thy pillow; and dream of me happily & sweetly.

May 16th, 1812.

I feel that every thing I had written in the way of amusements appears worthless and insipid when I think of one sweet smile of thy face, that I absolutely pant to behold it again.

May 30th, 1812.

What rapture is one soft smile from the heart (or rather from the soul), or a kiss from a lip of the wife & mother, even if time have somewhat impaired the freshness of her virgin beauties; what higher rapture is the consciousness that even for the pleasures of sense, the soul is triumphant through the might of sincere love, over the body; and that the mind can spread over the faded lips a more than youthful attraction, and preserve for the frame of the Beloved one an undying spirit of delight & tenderness ...

June 1st, 1812.

I came in last night wet and read both the Letters in bed. Thine was the tenderest & fondest of all I have yet received from thee, and my longing to have thee in my arms was so great, and the feelings of my heart so delicious, that my whole frame was over powered with Love & longing, Well was it for me that I was stretched upon my bed, for I think I could scarcely have stood upon my feet for excess of happiness & depth of affection.

...

Mary Wordsworth

Mary Wordsworth's letters to William Wordsworth were equally passionate. Here are some extracts.

August 1st, 1810.

O My William!
it is not in my power to tell thee how I have been affected by this dearest of all letters — it was so unexpected — so new a thing to see the breathing of thy inmost heart upon paper that I was quite overpowered, & now that I sit down to answer thee in the loneliness & depth of that love which unites us & which cannot be felt but by ourselves, I am so agitated & my eyes are so bedimmed that I scarcely know how to proceed.

May 23rd, 1812.

... instead of weakening, our union has strengthened — a hundred fold strengthened those yearnings towards each other ... that these feelings are mutual now, I have the fullest proof, from thy letters & from their power & the power of absence over my whole frame — Oh William I can not tell thee how I love thee, & thou must not desire it — but feel it, O feel it in the fullness of thy soul & *believe* that I am the happiest of Wives & of Mothers & of all Women the most blessed.

May 30th, 1812.

I am as happy as Woman can be wanting what constitutes that happiness — yet even *wanting this* I cannot but think that in the *thoughts* of my possessions I am the most blessed of all Women.

Ludwig van Beethoven

Ludwig van Beethoven (1770—1827), German composer, scribbled in pencil this letter to his 'Immortal Beloved' in 1811 or 1812. Beethoven never married. After his death the following letter was found amongst his belongings. The identity of the 'Immortal Beloved' has never been established beyond doubt; some experts believe she was Countess Josephine Deym, with whom Beethoven fell in love and to whom he wrote several love letters. Others favour Antonie von Brentano, who certainly knew Beethoven and lived near him in Vienna.

Though still in bed my thoughts go out to you, my Immortal Beloved, now and then joyfully, then sadly, waiting to learn whether or not fate will hear us. I can live only wholly with you or not at all — yes, I am resolved to wander so long away from you until I can fly to your arms and say that I am really at home, send my soul enwrapped in you into the land of spirits. — Yes, unhappily it must be so — you will be the more resolved since you know my fidelity — to you, no one can ever again possess my heart — none — never — Oh, God! why is it necessary to part from one whom one so loves and yet my life in Vienna is now a wretched life — your love makes me at once the happiest and the unhappiest of men — at my age, I need a steady, quiet life — can that be under our conditions? My angel, I have just been told that the mail coach goes every day — and I must close at once so that you may receive the L. at once. Be calm, only by a calm consideration of our existence can we achieve our purpose to live together — be calm — love me — to-day — yesterday — what tearful longings for you — you — you — my life — my all — farewell — Oh continue to love me — never misjudge the most faithful heart of your beloved L.
>
ever thine
ever mine
ever for each other

...

Heinrich von Kleist

Heinrich von Kleist (1777—1811), German dramatist and poet, wrote this letter to Adolfine Henriette Vogel, after Michaelmas, 1810. She was suffering from an incurable disease and the following year he killed both her and himself in a suicide pact.

My Jettchen, my little heart, my dear thing, my dovelet, my life, my dear sweet life, my life-light, my all, my goods and chattels, my castles, acres, lawns, and vineyards, O sun of my life, Sun, Moon, and Stars, Heaven and Earth, my Past and Future, my bride, my girl, my dear friend, my inmost being, my heart-blood, my entrails, star of my eyes, O dearest, what shall I call you?

My golden child, my pearl, my precious stone, my crown, my queen and empress. You dear darling of my heart, my highest and most precious, my all and everything, my wife, my wedding, the baptism of my children, my tragic play, my posthumous reputation. Ach! you are my second better self, my virtues, my merits, my hope, the forgiveness of my sins, my future and sanctity, O little daughter of Heaven, my child of God, my intercessor, my guardian angel, my Cherubim and Seraph, how I love you!

...

Gordon, Lord Byron

Gordon, Lord Byron (1788—1824), English poet, wrote this letter dated August 25th, 1819 to Teresa Guiccioli at the back of her copy of the novel *Corinne* by Madame de Staël. Guiccioli was a young Italian aristocrat married to a much older count. They lived together before he departed on his freedom-fighting mission to Greece, where he died of a fever.

My dearest Teresa,
I have read this book in your garden; — my love, you were absent, or else I could not have read it. It is a favourite book of yours, and the writer a friend of mine. You will not understand these English words, and *others* will not understand them, — which is the reason I have not scrawled them in Italian. But you will recognize the handwriting of him who passionately loved you, and you will divine that, over a book which was yours, he could only think of love.
In that word, beautiful in all languages, but most so in yours — *Amor mio* — is comprised my existence here and hereafter. I feel I exist here, and I feel I shall exist hereafter, — to *what* purpose you will decide; my destiny rests with you, and you are a woman, eighteen years of age, and two out of a convent, I wish that you had staid there, with all my heart, — or, at least, that I had never met you in your married state.
But this is too late. I love you, and you love me, — at least, you *say so*, and *act* as if you *did so*, which last is a great consolation in all events. But I more than love you, and cannot cease to love you.
Think of me, sometimes, when the Alps and ocean divide us, — but they never will, unless you *wish* it.

...

Percy Bysshe Shelley

Percy Bysshe Shelley (1792—1822), English poet, suffered agonies when separated from his great love, Mary Godwin, daughter of Mary Wollstonecraft. Shelley and Godwin were shunned by society when they eloped together, especially after his abandoned first wife committed suicide. He was forced to hide from his creditors and they could only meet secretly in coffee shops and graveyards. They eventually fled to the continent and were married. Shelley drowned in a boating accident in Italy at the age of 30. These letters were written on October 27th and 28th, 1814, when Shelley was in hiding.

Oh my dearest love why are our pleasures so short & interrupted? How long is this to last? — Know you my best Mary that I feel myself in your absence almost degraded to the level of the vulgar & impure.

I feel their vacant stiff eyeballs fixed upon me — until I seem to have been infected with loathsome meaning — to inhale a sickness that subdues me to languor. Oh! those redeeming eyes of Mary that they might beam upon me before I sleep! Praise my forbearance oh beloved one that I do not rashly fly to you — & at least secure a *moments* bliss — Wherefore should I delay — do you not long to meet me? All that is exalted & buoyant in my nature urges me towards you — reproaches me with cold delay — laughs at all fear & spurns to dream of prudence! Why am I not with you? — Alas we must not meet.

October 28th, 1814.

Mary love — we must be united. I will not part from you again after Saturday night. We must devise some scheme. I must return. Your thoughts alone can waken mine to energy. My mind without yours is dead & cold as the dark midnight river when the moon is down. It seems as if you alone could shield me from impurity & vice. If I were absent from you long I should shudder with horror at myself. My understanding becomes undisciplined without you. I believe I must become in Marys hands what Harriet was in mine — yet how differently disposed how devoted & affectionate: how beyond measure reverencing & adoring the intelligence that governs me — I repent me of this simile it is unjust — it is false. Nor do I mean that I consider you much my superior — evidently as you surpass me in originality & simplicity of mind. —How divinely sweet a task it is to imitate each others excellencies — & each moment to become wiser in this surpassing love ...

...

John Keats

John Keats (1795—1821), English poet, first met Fanny Brawne in 1818 and they formed an understanding in December of that year. They lived next door to each other and then in the same house during 1819 and 1820, but Keats's obsessiveness and ill-health doomed the relationship from the start. The poet died in 1821 in Rome, where he had gone seeking warmth to ease his tuberculosis. Letters from Fanny

Brawne were buried with him. Here are extracts from his letters to her.

July 1st, 1819.

Ask yourself my love whether you are not very cruel to have so entrammelled me, so destroyed my freedom. Will you confess this in the Letter you must write immediately and do all you can to console me in it — make it rich as a draught of poppies to intoxicate me — write the softest words and kiss them that I may at least touch my lips where yours have been ... I almost wish we were butterflies and liv'd but three summer days — three such days with you I could fill with more delight than fifty common years could ever contain.

July 8th, 1819.

Your Letter gave me more delight, than any thing in the world but yourself could do; indeed I am almost astonished that any absent one should have that luxurious power over my senses which I feel. Even when I am not thinking of you I receive your influence and a tenderer nature steeling upon me. All my thoughts, my unhappiest days and nights have I find not at all cured me of my love of Beauty, but made it so intense that I am miserable that you are not with me: or rather breathe in that dull sort of patience that cannot be called Life. I never knew before, what such a love as you have made me feel, was; I did not believe in it; my Fancy was afraid of it, lest it should burn me up.

But if you will fully love me, though there may be some fire, 'twill not be more than we can bear when moistened and bedewed with Pleasures ... I would never see any thing but Pleasure in your eyes, love on your lips, and Happiness in your steps.

August 5th, 1819.

I have two luxuries to brood over in my walks, your Loveliness and the hour of my death. O that I could have possession of them both in the same minute. I hate the world: it batters too much the wings of my self-will, and would I could take a sweet poison from your lips to send me out of it.

March 1820.

You fear, sometimes, I do not love you so much as you wish? My dear Girl I love you ever and ever and without reserve. The more I have known you the more have I lov'd. In every way — even my jealousies have been agonies of Love, in the hottest fit I ever had I would have died for you. I have vex'd you too much. But for Love!

41

Can I help it?

You are always new. The last of your kisses was ever the sweetest; the last smile the brightest; the last movement the gracefullest. When you pass'd my window home yesterday, I was fill'd with as much admiration as if I had then seen you for the first time. You uttered a half complaint once that I only lov'd your Beauty. Have I nothing else then to love in you but that? Do not I see a heart naturally furnish'd with wings imprison itself with me?

...

Alexander Pushkin

Alexander Pushkin (1799—1837), Russian writer, sent this letter to Anna Petrovna Kern on December 8th, 1825. She was married to someone else, but until his own marriage in 1831, Pushkin never let his mistresses' husbands get in the way of his urgent romances. This led to more than one duel.

I little expected, enchantress, that you would remember me; from the bottom of my soul I thank you for doing so. Byron has just acquired a new charm for me — all his heroines will assume unforgettable features in my imagination. I shall see you in *Gulnare* and in *Leila* — the ideal one of Byron himself could not be more divine. So it is you, always you, that fate sends to enchant my solitude! You are the angel of consolation — but I am only an ingrate, for I still complain ... You are going to Petersburg; my exile weighs on me more than ever. Perhaps the change which has just taken place will bring me closer to you; I do not dare to hope so. Let us not believe in hope; she is only a pretty woman who treats us like old husbands. What is yours doing, my sweet genie? Do you know, I imagine the enemies of Byron, including his wife, as having his features.

I take my pen again to tell you that I am at your knees, that I still love you, that I detest you sometimes, that the day before yesterday I said horrible things about you, that I kiss your beautiful hands, that I kiss them again pending something better, that I am at the end of my tether, that you are divine, etc.

...

Honoré de Balzac

Honoré de Balzac (1799—1850), French writer, fell irrevocably in love with Evelina Hanska, a Polish countess. They agreed to postpone the ultimate fulfilment of their love until the death of her elderly husband. After many years of passionate correspondence, haunted by frustration and insecurities, the couple finally married in 1850. Ironically, Balzac survived his wedding day by only a few months.

June 1st, 1833.

Excuse my scrawlings. My heart and my head always go quicker than anything else, and when I am writing to a woman I love, I very often become illegible.

October 6th, 1833.

... it will bloom always fairer, fresher, more gracious, because it is a true love, and because genuine love is ever increasing. It is a beautiful plant growing from year to year in the heart, ever extending its palms and branches, doubling every season its glorious clusters and perfumes; and, my dear life, tell me, repeat to me always, that nothing will bruise its bark or its delicate leaves, that it will grow larger in both our hearts, loved, free, watched over, like a life within our life ...

January 1834.

Do you remember the bird that has only one flower? That is the history of my heart and of my love. O dear, heavenly flower, dear balmy perfumes, dear fresh colours, my beautiful stem, do not bend! protect me always! At every progressive step of a love which goes, which will go on always increasing, I feel in my heart household fires of tenderness and adoration. Oh! I wish I could be as sure of you as I am of myself. I feel with every breath I draw that I have a constancy in my heart which nothing will change.

January 1834.

God in heaven! how am I to tell you that I am intoxicated with the faintest odour of you, that, had I possessed you a thousand times, you would see me still more intoxicated, because there would be hope and memory where there is as yet only hope.

...

Juliette Drouet

Juliette Drouet, French actress, gave up the stage to devote herself to Victor Hugo, the French writer. She saved his life during the uprisings of 1851. They were lovers for 50 years, and she followed him into dreary political exile on Jersey, living in the house next door to Hugo and his official household. Every morning she sent her lover two soft-boiled eggs and a love letter. A large body of Drouet's correspondence has survived, and it is considered by many to be the most beautiful collection of love letters in the French language. Drouet was obliged to share Hugo not just with his wife, but also with other mistresses. Hugo even forced her to take part in a contest of devotion with another long-term lover, Léonie D'Aunet. Drouet won

43

convincingly with her delectable, self-effacing prose. Here are some extracts.

1833.

I love you *because* I love you, because it would be impossible for me not to love you. I love you without question, without calculation, without reason good or bad, faithfully, with all my heart and soul, and every faculty. Believe it, for it is true. If you cannot believe, I being at your side, I will make a drastic effort to force you to do so. I shall have the mournful satisfaction of sacrificing myself utterly to a distrust as absurd as it is unfounded.

1835.

There can be no happiness greater than that I enjoyed this afternoon with you, clasped in your arms, your voice mingling with mine, your eyes in mine, your heart upon my heart, our very souls welded together. For me, there is no man on this earth but you. The others I perceive only through your love. I enjoy nothing without you. You are the prism through which the sunshine, the green landscape, and life itself, appear to me ...
 I do not know how to employ either my body or my soul, away from you. I only come to life again in your presence. I need your kisses upon my lips, your love in my soul.

September 1845.

I have just been gardening, beloved. I am soaked with dew and all muddy, but I have spent three hours thinking of you without any bitterness. My eyes were as moist as my flowers, but I was not weeping. While I busied myself with the garden, I reviewed in thought the lovely flowers of my past happiness. I saw them again fresh and blooming as the first day, and I felt close to you, separated only by a breath. As long as the illusion lasted I was almost happy. I should have liked to pluck my soul and send it to you as a nosegay.

...

Victor Hugo

Victor Hugo (1802—85) also exchanged many letters with his wife, Adèle Foucher. The couple were childhood sweethearts but their union was forbidden by her parents for two wretched years. However, Hugo prevailed in the end and they were married on October 12th, 1822. Foucher eventually destroyed her part of the correspondence, possibly finding it devalued by Hugo's voluminous output of love letters to other women, especially Juliette Drouet. Here is a taste of those letters.

January 1820.

Yes, you can do anything with me; and to-morrow, were I even dead, the sweet tones of your voice, the tender pressure of your lips, would call me back to life again.

October 1820.

Ah! my Adèle, love me as I love you, and I will take care for all the rest.

October 20th, 1821.

The soul, so superior to the body to which it is bound, would remain on earth in intolerable solitude, if it were not allowed to some extent to choose from among all the souls of other men a partner to share with it misery in this life and bliss in eternity. When two souls, which have sought each other for however long in the throng, have finally found each other, when they have seen that they are matched, are in sympathy and compatible, in a word, that they are alike, there is then established for ever between them a union, fiery and pure as they themselves are, a union which begins on earth and continues for ever in heaven. This union is love, true love, such as in truth very few men can conceive of, that love which is a religion, which deifies the loved one, whose life comes from devotion and passion, and for which the greatest sacrifices are the sweetest delights. This is the love which you inspire in me.

...

Nathaniel Hawthorne

Nathaniel Hawthorne (1804—64), American writer, author of *The Scarlet Letter*, enjoyed a lyrical romance with Sophia Peabody. They were married on July 9th, 1842 and the happy love affair continued throughout their marriage, despite financial difficulties and Peabody's frail constitution. She retrospectively censored some of their early love letters as she felt they showed too much passion for an unmarried couple.

March 6th, 1839.

It almost seems to me, now, as if beautiful days were wasted and thrown away, when we do not feel their beauty and heavenliness through one another.

August 8th, 1839.

Did you not know, beloved, that I dreamed of you, as it seemed to me, all night long, after that last blissful meeting? It is true, when I looked back upon the dream, it immediately became confused; but it had been vivid, and most happy, and left a sense of happiness in my heart. Come again, sweet wife! Force your way through the mists and vapors that envelope my slumbers — illumine me with a radiance that shall not vanish when I awake. I throw my heart as wide open to you as I can. Come and rest within it, my Dove. Where else should you rest at night, if not in your husband's arms — and quite securely in his heart.

September 23rd, 1839.

My little Dove, I have observed that butterflies — very broad-winged and magnificent butterflies — frequently come on board of the salt ships where I am at work. What have these bright strangers to do on Long Wharf, where there are no flowers nor any green thing — nothing but brick stores, stone piers, black ships, and the bustle of toilsome men, who neither look up to the blue sky, nor take note of these wandering gems of air. I cannot account for them, unless, dearest, they are the lovely fantasies of your mind, which you send thither in search of me.

...

Elizabeth Barrett and Robert Browning

The English poets Elizabeth Barrett (1806—61) and Robert Browning (1812—89) exchanged hundreds of letters before eloping to Italy in 1845. They lived in great happiness until Barrett's death. Browning wrote this loving 'fan' letter to his future wife on January 10th, 1845 — before he had even met her.

I love your verses with all my heart, dear Miss Barrett, — and this is no off-hand complimentary letter that I shall write, — whatever else, no prompt matter-of-course recognition of your genius and there a graceful and natural end of the thing: since the day last week when I first read your poems, I quite laugh to remember how I have been turning and turning again in my mind what I should be able to tell you of their effect upon me — for in the first flush of delight I thought I would this once get out of my habit of purely passive enjoyment, when I do really enjoy, and thoroughly justify my admiration — perhaps even, as a loyal fellow-craftsman should, try and find fault and do you some little good to be proud of hereafter! — but nothing comes of it all — so into me has it gone, and part of me has it become, this great living poetry of yours, not a flower of which but took root and grew ... oh, how different that is from lying to be dried and pressed flat and prized highly and put in a book with a proper account at top and bottom, and shut up and put away ... and the book called a 'Flora,' besides! After all, I need not give up the thought of doing that, too, in time; because even now, talking with whoever is worthy, I can give a reason for my faith in one and another excellence, the fresh strange music, the affluent language, the exquisite pathos and true new brave thought — but in this addressing myself to you, your own self, and for the first time, my feeling rises altogether. I do, as I say, love these Books with all my heart — and I love you too: do you know I was once not very far from seeing ... really seeing you? Mr Kenyon said to me one morning 'would you like to see Miss Barrett?' — then he went to announce me, — then he returned ... you were too unwell — and now it is years ago — and I feel as at some untoward passage in my travels — as if I had been close, so close, to some world's-wonder in chapel or crypt, ... only a screen to push and I might have entered — but there was some slight ... so now it seems ... slight and just-sufficient bar to admission, and the half-opened door shut, and I went home my thousands of miles, and the sight was never to be!

Well, these Poems were to be — and this true thankful joy and pride with which I feel myself,

Yours ever faithfully

Robert Browning

...

Edgar Allan Poe

Edgar Allan Poe (1809—49), American writer, wrote this tremulous declaration to Sarah Helen Whitman, American poet, on October 1st, 1848. His wife had died the previous year, and the distraught Poe wrote feverish letters to both Whitman and a married woman, Anne Richmond. He had just a year to live, destroyed by alcohol and depression.

All thoughts — all passions seem now merged in that one consuming desire — the mere wish to make you comprehend — to make you see *that* for which there is no human voice — the unutterable fervor of my love for you ... but if, throughout some long, dark summer night, I could but have held you close, close to my heart and whispered to you the strange secrets of its passionate history, then indeed you would have seen that I have been far from attempting to deceive you in this respect. I could have shown you that it was not and could never have been in the power of any other than yourself to move me as I am now moved — to oppress me with this ineffable emotion — to surround and bathe me in this electric light, illumining and enkindling my whole nature — filling my soul with glory, with wonder, and with awe ...

Do you not feel in your inmost heart of hearts that the 'soul-love' of which the world speaks so often and so idly is, in this instance at least, but the veriest, the most absolute of realities? Do you not — I ask it of your reason, *darling*, not less than of your heart — do you not perceive that it is my diviner nature — my spiritual being — which burns and pants to commingle with your own? ...

Have I not *seen* you, Helen? Have I not heard the more than melody of your voice? Has not my heart ceased to throb beneath the magic of your smile? Have I not held your hand in mine and looked steadily into your soul through the crystal Heaven of your eyes? Have I not done all these things? — or do I dream? — or am I mad? ... Who *ever* saw you and did not love? ...

My soul, this night, shall come to you in dreams and speak to you those fervid thanks which my pen is all powerless to utter.

...

Robert Schumann

Robert Schumann (1810—56), German composer, fell in love with Clara Wieck, a German pianist. Wieck's ambitious father did everything he could to thwart the match, which he saw as detrimental to his daughter's brilliant career. But Schumann eventually prevailed and the couple were married in 1840. Schumann unfortunately succumbed to schizophrenia in the 1850s and ended his days in an asylum.

September 18th, 1837.

The interview with your father was terrible. Such coldness, such malice, such distraction, such contradictions — he has a new way of destroying one, he thrusts the knife into your heart up to the hilt ... So what now, dearest Clara? I cannot tell what to do next ... Above all, arm yourself, and *do not let yourself be sold* ... I trust you, oh *with my whole heart*, indeed that is what sustains me — but you will have to be *very strong*, more than you have any idea. For your father gave me with his own lips the dreadful assurance that 'nothing would shake him' ... Today I feel so dead, so humiliated, that I can scarcely grasp one beautiful, pleasant thought; even your picture eludes me, so that I can scarcely remember your eyes. I have not grown faint-hearted, capable of giving you up; but so embittered, so offended in my most sacred feelings ...

April 15th, 1838.

What would I not do for love of you, my own Clara! The knights of old were better off; they could go through fire or slay dragons to win their ladies, but we of today have to content ourselves with more prosaic methods, such as smoking fewer cigars, and the like.

After all, though, we can love, knights or no knights; and so, as ever, only the times change, not men's hearts.

March 30th, 1840.

A month to-day I shall be with you, God willing, dear child. Shall you not be happy to feel my arms about you again? Will you arrange a little private concert for your lover? I should like the big sonata in B flat (the whole of it), then one of my own songs, played and sung by yourself (the words are the chief thing, remember), then your new scherzo, and, to wind up, Bach's C sharp minor fugue from the second book. It is not to be a charity concert! I am prepared to pay liberally. We shall settle our accounts at the end — you can guess in what coin. How I shall look forward to this lovers' recital! You dearest, best of creatures, I shall smother you with kisses when I see you.

...

Alfred de Musset

Alfred de Musset (1810—57), French writer, authored this melodramatic appeal to his lover and fellow writer, George Sand (Amantine Aurore Dudevant). The imperious, impulsive Sand abandoned the weak, whining and drunken de Musset when she fell in love with Doctor Pietro Pagello while the couple were visiting Venice. A lengthy and, in some ways, grotesquely funny emotional blackmailing by de Musset ensued. Each of the two writers also created their own thinly disguised fictional accounts of their frenzied love affair, which quite possibly generated more melodrama and purple prose than real passion. De Musset's *Confessions d'un Enfant du Siècle* painted a bitter portrait of his mistress. George Sand's own *Elle et Lui* attempted to put the record straight 30 years later. De Musset's brother instantly responded with his own book, *Lui et Elle*, and the whole affair was then satirized by Gaston Lavalley in his novel *Eux*. This letter was written in August 1834, after de Musset and Sand had made a tender parting.

I send you a last farewell, my well-beloved, and I send it to you with confidence, not without grief, but without despair. The cruel agonies, the poignant struggles, the bitter tears have been replaced by a tender companion, pale and gentle Melancholy. This morning, after a tranquil night, I found her at my bedside, with a sweet smile on her lips. This is the friend that will go with me. She bears your last kiss on her forehead. Why should I fear to tell you so? Was it not as chaste, as pure as your beautiful soul, oh my well-beloved? You will never reproach yourself with those two sad hours that we have passed together. You will keep the memory of them. They were poured on my wounds like a healing balm. You will never repent having left to your poor friend a memory that he will carry like a talisman between the world and himself, during all the pains and joys of the future. Our love is consecrated, my child; yesterday it received, before God, the holy baptism of our tears. It is immortal as He is. I neither hope nor fear any more. I have done with the earth. No greater happiness is in store for me. Oh, my cherished sister, I am leaving my country, my mother, my friends, the world where I spent my youth, I go away alone, for ever, and I thank God. He that is loved by you can no longer curse. George, I can still suffer now, but I can no longer curse. As to our future relations, you alone shall decide all that regards my life, speak, say the word, my child, my life is yours.

Write to me that I must go and die in silence in a corner of the earth, three hundred leagues away from you and I will do it. Consult your heart, if you believe that God tells you to do so, cease to defend our poor friendship, only send me from time to time a handclasp, a word, a tear — all, these are my only blessings. But if you believe that you must sacrifice our friendship, if my letters, sent even from beyond France, trouble your happiness, or only your repose, do not hesitate to forget me. I tell you that I can suffer much, at present, without complaining. Be happy at all costs. Oh, be happy, well-beloved of my soul! Time is inexorable, Death is avaricious, and the last years of youth pass more quickly than do the first. Be happy, but, if you cannot, forget that happiness is possible. Yesterday you told me that you had never been so! What did I reply? I do not know, alas! It is not for me to speak of this. Those condemned to death do not deny their God. Be happy, be brave, have patience, have pity. Try to vanquish a just pride. Restrain your heart, my noble George, you have too much heart for a human bosom. But if you renounce life, if you ever find yourself alone in face of unhappiness, recall the vow that you made me — 'I will not die without you.' Remember that, remember that, you promised it to me before God.

But I shall not die, no, not without having written my book, on myself, on you — you above all, no, my beautiful, my sainted betrothed, you shall not rest beneath the cold earth before that earth knows what it has borne. No, no, I swear by my youth and my genius, only stainless lilies shall grow on your tomb. I with these hands will place a marble to bear your epitaph— a marble whiter than the statues of our glories of a day. Posterity will repeat our names together with those of immortal lovers who were as one, as Romeo and Juliet, Héloïse and Abelard. They will never speak of one without the other. This will be a marriage more sacred and chaste than any that the priests make, the imperishable marriage of Intelligence …

Ah George, what love! Man has never loved as I love you. I am lost, understand that, I am drowned, swamped in love; I no longer know if I live, if I eat, if I walk, if I breathe, if I speak; I only know that I love. Ah, if all your life you have had a yearning for inexhaustible happiness, if it is a happiness to be loved, if you have ever asked this love of Heaven, oh, my life, my blessing, my well-beloved, look at the sun, the flowers, the grass, all the world, and know that you are loved, as all these will tell you, loved as God might be by his Levites, his saints, his martyrs! I love you, oh, my flesh and my blood! I die of love, of an endless nameless love, an insensate, desperate lost love! You are loved, adored, idolized till death! No, I shall never be cured, no, I shall not try to live, I love better than that, to die loving you is worth more than living. I know well enough what they are saying. They say that you have another lover. I know it well, I die of it, but I love, I love, I love.

...

Franz Liszt

Franz Liszt (1811—86), Hungarian composer and piano virtuoso, became enamoured of Countess Marie d'Agoult, French woman of letters. She left her husband, children and grand lifestyle to elope with Liszt. Their passionate union resulted in three daughters, one of whom was to become Cosima Wagner. The couple parted in 1844, when Liszt's craving for fame tempted him away from their secluded life. There was also competition for his romantic attention, and d'Agoult, once described as 'six inches of snow covering twenty feet of lava', was prepared to be his mistress, but not one of his mistresses. Under the pseudonym Daniel Stern, d'Agoult wrote plays, novels, memoirs and a highly respected account of the 1848 revolution. This letter to her was written in 1834.

My heart overflows with emotion and joy! I do not know what heavenly languor, what infinite pleasure permeates it and burns me up. It is as if I had never loved!!! Tell me whence these uncanny disturbances spring, these inexpressible foretastes of delight, these divine tremors of love. Oh! all this can only spring from you, sister, angel, woman, Marie! ... All this can only be, is surely nothing less than a gentle ray streaming from your fiery soul, or else some secret poignant teardrop which you have long since left in my breast.

My God, my God, never force us apart, take pity on us! But what am I saying? Forgive my weakness, how couldst Thou divide us! Thou wouldst have nothing but pity for us ... No, no! ... It is not in vain that our flesh and our souls quicken and become immortal through Thy Word, which cries out deep within us Father, Father ... it is not in vain that Thou callest us, that Thou reachest out Thine hand to us, that our broken hearts seek their refuge in Thee ... O! we thank, bless and praise Thee, O God, for all that Thou hast given us, and all that Thou prepared for us ...

This is to be — to be!

Marie! Marie!

Oh let me repeat that name a hundred times, a thousand times over; for three days now it has lived within me, oppressed me, set me afire. I am not writing to you, no, I am close beside you. I see you, I hear you ... Eternity in your arms ... Heaven, Hell, everything, all is within you, redoubled ... Oh! Leave me free to rave in my delirium. Drab, tame, constricting reality is no longer enough for me. We must live our lives to the full, loving and suffering to extremes! ... Oh! you believe me capable of self-sacrifice, chastity, temperance and piety, do you not? But let no more be said of this ... it is up to you to question, to draw conclusions, to save me as you see fit. Leave me free to rave in my delirium, since you can do nothing, nothing at all for me.

This is to be! to be!!!

...

Charlotte Brontë

Charlotte Brontë (1816—55), English writer, was employed by Professor Constantin Héger as a governess for his children in Belgium. She fell hopelessly in love with him. Madame Héger was hostile, and Charlotte returned to England. Her passion for Héger was not, apparently, returned, and nor were her heart-rending letters to him. In between letters, she 'fasted', in other words, she refrained from writing to him for months at a time. These periods of epistolary celibacy were productive in other ways. She wrote a novel, called *The Professor*, which remained unpublished until after her death, but also her celebrated novel, *Jane Eyre,* about a humble orphan who fell in love with her darkly glamorous — but, as it turned out, married — employer. Brontë's love poems from this period also reveal a terrible emotional abandonment.

January 8th, 1845.

Monsieur, the poor have not need of much to sustain them — they ask only for the crumbs that fall from the rich men's table. But if they are refused the crumbs they die of hunger. Nor do I, either, need much affection from those I love. I should not know what to do with a friendship entire and complete — I am not used to it. But you showed me of yore a little interest, when I was your pupil in Brussels, and I hold on to the maintenance of that little interest — I hold on to it as I would hold on to life.

November 18th, 1846.

To forbid me to write to you, to refuse to answer me, would be to tear from me my only joy on earth, to deprive me of my last privilege ... when a prolonged and gloomy silence seems to threaten me with the estrangement of my master — when day by day I await a letter, and when day by day disappointment comes to fling me back into overwhelming sorrow, and the sweet delight of seeing your handwriting and reading your counsel escapes me as a vision that is vain, then fever claims me — I lose appetite and sleep — I pine away.

...

John Ruskin

John Ruskin (1819—1900), English writer, artist, designer and philosopher, conducted a breathless, fearful courtship with his future wife, Euphemia ('Effie') Gray, which ended disastrously. The couple were totally incompatible in interests and intellect. The marriage was never consummated. Gray left him and married another English painter, Sir John Everett Millais, by whom she had eight children.

November 21st, 1847.

I have been thinking how long it will be before I know all your letters by heart. Not long — Yet I should so like to have them printed, in a little pocket volume — to carry about with me always.

January 19th, 1848.

I don't regret our little quarrels, now; I think even at the time there was a kind of luxury in them — I don't know what it was — but I cannot help suspecting myself — now and then — of having in some slight degree, made matters worse for the sake of the delight of making friends again. Do you think we shall be able to quarrel in that sort of amateur fashion at Bowers Well. I'm afraid not — I don't think I could even *play* a quarrel — now. I am quite passive — in your power — you may do what you will with me — if you were to put me into *Bowers Well* and put the top on, I should think it was all right, and the kindest thing in the world. You said I was cross the other day — peut-être — but in the first place I was more anxious than cross — and in the second place — I don't profess to be in a good humour when I am away from you — A little thing puts me out now — but when I once get near you — Ah. what will become of me. I shall have no more independent existence than your shadow has — I feel as if I should faint away for love of you — and become a mist or a smoke, like the Genie in the Arabian nights — and as if the best you could do with me would be to get me all folded and gathered into a little box — and put on your toilet-table — and let me out a little now and then — when I wouldn't be troublesome.

March 13th, 1848.

I am *very* sorry my wicked letter made you sad — and yet selfishly glad I wrote it — and the naughty one before it too. — since they have obtained for me two such lovely letters to conclude the sweet series which I have of gentle and forgiving and loving and rejoicing — and comforting expression of your kind heart — many a kiss have I given to the letter of Saturday — and a joyous evening I had. I could not get away — for we had company, but I stole a moment at the fireside in the dining-room, and saw the first page and those closing words — and if you could but have felt my poor heart leaping for joy.

...

Gustave Flaubert

Gustave Flaubert (1821—80), French writer, based the character of his fictional heroine Madame Bovary on his lover, the French poet Louise Colet. The couple raged through two stormy love affairs in the 1840s and 1850s. Flaubert ended two years of celibacy the day he met Colet, who was modelling in the studio of the sculptor James Pradier. But Flaubert was unable to commit and Colet was unable to compromise. He finally rejected her, and is thought to have burned her letters to him — a great loss to epistolary history. Colet was a formidable siren. Another of her lovers, Alfred de Musset, described her as a 'Venus of hot marble'. These are extracts from two letters written on August 9th, 1846.

I keep dreaming of your face, of your shoulders, of your white neck, of your smile, of your voice that's like a love-cry, impassioned, violent, and sweet all at once ...

Before I knew you I was calm; I had become so ... Then you came along, and with the mere touch of a fingertip you threw everything into confusion. The old dregs boiled up again; the lake of my heart began to churn. But only the ocean has tempests; ponds, when they are stirred up, produce nothing but unhealthy smells. I must love you to tell you this. Forget me if you can, tear your soul from your body with your two hands and trample on it, to destroy the traces of me that are in it ...

I'll try to arrive some evening about six. We'll have all night and the next day. We'll set the night ablaze! I'll be your desire, you'll be mine, and we'll gorge ourselves on each other to see whether we can be satiated. Never! No, never! Your heart is an inexhaustible spring, you let me drink deep, it floods me, penetrates me, I drown. Oh! The beauty of your face, all pale and quivering beneath my kisses ... Adieu, I kiss you in the place where I *will* kiss you, where I wanted to; I place my mouth there. I roll on you. A thousand kisses. Oh, give me some! Give me some!

What irresistible impulse drove me toward you? For an instant I saw the abyss. I realized its depth and then vertigo swept me over ...

Adieu, my darling; I have just gone down into the garden and gathered this little rose which I am sending you. I kiss it; put it quickly to your mouth, and then — you know where ... Adieu! A thousand kisses. I am yours from night to day, from day to night.

...

Mark Twain

Mark Twain (Samuel Langhorne Clemens) (1835—1910), American writer, was the author of *The Adventures of Tom Sawyer* and *The Adventures of Huckleberry Finn*. He romanced Olivia Langdon, his future wife, with loving, cheerful letters, like the following ones written in 1869.

March 6th, 1869.

Livy, dear, I have already mailed to-day's letter, but I am so proud of my privilege of writing the dearest girl in the world whenever I please, that I must add a few lines if only to say *I love you*, Livy. For I *do* love you, Livy — as the dew loves the flowers; as the birds love the sunshine; as the wavelets love the breeze; as mothers love their first-born, as memory loves old faces, as the yearning tides love the moon; as the angels love the pure in heart. I so love you that if you were taken from me it seems as if all my love would follow after you & leave my heart a dull & vacant ruin forever & forever. And so loving you I do also honor you, as never vassal, leal & true, honoured sceptred king since this good world of ours began. And now that is honest, & I think you ought to reach up & give me a kiss, Livy. (Or will I stoop down to your dainty little altitude, very willingly, for such a guerdon.)

May 12th, 1869.

From the stillness that reigns in the house, I fancy that I must be the only person up, though I know it is not late. However, the very dearest girl in the wide world has given me strict orders to go to bed early & take care of myself, & I will obey, though I had rather

The World's Greatest Letters

write to her than sleep — for, writing to her, it is as if I were *talking* to her — & to talk to her so, is in fancy to hold her tiny hand, & look into her dear eyes, & hear her voice that is sweet as an answered prayer to me, & clasp her pigmy foot, & hold her dainty form in my arms, & kiss her lips & cheeks, & hair & eyes for love, & her sacred forehead in honor, in reverent respect, in gratitude & blessing. Out of the depths of my happy heart wells a great tide of love & prayer for this priceless treasure that is confided to my life-long keeping. You cannot see its intangible waves as they flow toward you, darling, but in these lines you will hear, as it were, the distant beating of its surf.

I leave you with the ministering spirits that are in the air about you always. Good-night, with a kiss & a blessing, Livy darling.

...

Sarah Bernhardt

Sarah Bernhardt (1844—1923), French actress, was a legendary figure in the theatre world and the greatest *tragédienne* of her day. Many of her love letters have survived, including these ones to Jean Richepin, French poet, adventurer and dramatist, written some time in 1883. She was not able to keep her promises of fidelity and he was not able to tolerate her failure to do so.

My adored, my maddening master, I ask you to pardon me. Oh yes! A great pardon. What I said to you must have been unspeakably vile since you write me in such a howling rage ... Yes, I know that I like to deceive, that I am made of evil thoughts and betrayals. I deserve every bad name you choose to call me ...

I fondle your adored body, I kiss your every hair — and my lips demand that your lips forgive me a thousand times.

A further letter to Richepin, the same year:

I behaved badly only because I felt superior to all who surround me. That is over. You appeared. You blew your powerful breath on my lies, and my equivocal 'maybes' and 'becauses' were blown away. I drank the truth of love from your lips, and, quivering in your arms, I felt the real, the wild sensations of the body's ecstasy, and I saw in your eyes the absolute supremacy of your being. I gave myself to you completely ... and completely new — for I brought you a being that belonged to you and you alone. I did not invent anything about myself. Indeed, I rediscovered myself in you ... You left me without giving me time to think, while I was still moist from your arms, still perfumed by the intoxicating scent of your

56

body. I looked at our bed, thought of our night together, our awakening, our embraces ...

and in 1884:

Yes, yes, I was bad the other day. Oh, how I weep for that badness in me. How I regret having spoken evil words that you think of now that you are alone. Oh, my adored lover, my beloved idol, my seigneur, think only of the sweet, tender words I've said to you, my prince, of my absolute passion, my adoration, my devotion. I no longer have any pride. I am tamed! I am at your feet, submissive and repentant. Never, never again will I be bad.

...

August Strindberg

August Strindberg (1849—1912), Swedish dramatist, fell deeply in love with an actress, Harriet Bosse, who became his third wife. Bosse was many years his junior. They separated a year after the birth of their daughter, and in most of his later letters he pleaded with her to come back to him. Bosse was one of Scandinavia's great actresses and frequently acted in his plays. At their first meeting, Strindberg had begged a feather from her hat to use as a writing quill. This letter is dated April 28th, 1901.

Beloved,
You ask if you can impart something good and beautiful to my life! And yet — what have you not already given me?
When you, my dearly beloved, my friend, stepped into my home three months ago, I was griefstricken, old and ugly — almost hardened and irreclaimable, lacking in hope.
And then you came!
What happened?
First you made me almost good!
Then you gave me back my youth!
And after that, you awakened in me a hope for a better life!
And you taught me that there is beauty in life — in moderation ... and you taught me the beauty of poetic imagery — *Swanwhite!* ...
You have taught me to speak with purity, to speak beautiful words. You have taught me to think loftily and with high purpose. You have taught me to forgive an enemy. You have taught me to have reverence for the fates of others and not only my own.

...

Woodrow Wilson

Woodrow Wilson (1856—1924), 28th President of the United States, wrote this letter to his future wife, Ellen Axson Wilson, on June 21st, 1885. Their marriage, as witnessed by their beautiful love letters to each other, was exceptionally loving and harmonious.

It seems altogether too good to be true that our bondage to pen and paper is at last at an end! ... This letter will reach you on Monday, and on Tuesday I shall go to my darling to carry the words of love with which my heart is so full ... to consecrate to her my life, that it may be spent in making perfect the fulfilment of all the sweet promises in which our love for each other is so rich. Ah, my sweetheart, I wish that I could show you *some* of the gladness with which these thoughts fill me. But it is literally unspeakable. It is not translatable into anything but high spirits and a tumultuous throbbing at the heart ...

...

Ellen Axson Wilson

Ellen Axson Wilson to Woodrow Wilson, May 11th, 1886.

It is my *deliberate* belief that no one else in the world is as happy as I am and have been since the day I was wed; that scarcely anyone else could be made to believe such happiness was possible. I could not believe it one year ago ... It is like the joys of Heaven which the strongest imagination is unable to reveal to us — until we attain them they are altogether hidden from us. But you, darling, have made an earthly paradise for me.

...

George Bernard Shaw

George Bernard Shaw (1856—1950), Irish dramatist, conducted a rambunctious correspondence with the English actress Mrs Patrick Campbell. 'Stella' was his nickname for her. The letters, as these extracts show, were full of literary bravura.

December 10th, 1912.

Oh, before you go, my Stella, I clasp you to my heart 'with such a strained purity.' A thousand successes, a thousand healings, a thousand braveries, a thousand prayers, a thousand beauties, a thousand hopes and faiths and loves and adorations watch over you and rain upon you. Goodnight, goodnight, goodnight, goodnight, my dearest dearest.

February 27th, 1913.

I want my rapscallionly fellow vagabond. I want my dark lady. I want my angel — I want my tempter. I want my Freia with her apples. I want the lighter of my seven lamps of beauty, honour, laughter, music, love, life and immortality ...

I want my inspiration, my folly, my happiness, my divinity, my madness, my selfishness, my final sanity and sanctification, my transfiguration, my purification, my light across the sea, my palm across the desert, my garden of lovely flowers, my million nameless joys, my day's wage, my night's dream, my darling and my star ...

O cruel, cruel, cruel, cruel, have you no heart at all?

July 18th, 1913.

There is a woman there whom I love, a most wonderfully beautiful and utterly frank and simple woman; and I'll drag her out and adore her, no matter how many bundles of rags and bags of tricks you hide her in.

December 31st, 1913.

... for you have wakened the latent tragedy in me, broken through my proud overbearing gaiety that carried all the tragedies of the world like feathers and stuck them in my cap and laughed. And if your part in it was an illusion, then I am as lonely as God. Therefore you must still be the Mother of Angels to me, still from time to time put on your divinity and sit in the heavens with me. For that, with all our assumed cleverness and picked up arts to stave off the world, is all we two are really fit for. Remember this always — even when we are grovelling and racketing and drudging; for in this remembrance I am deeply faithful to you — faithful beyond all love. Be faithful to me in it and I will forgive you though you betray me in everything else — forgive you, bless you, honour you, and adore you. *Super hanc stellum* will I build my church.

And now let us again hear the bells ring: you on your throne in your blue hood, and I watching and praying, not on my knees, but at my fullest stature. For you I wear my head nearest the skies.

...

Gustav Mahler

Gustav Mahler (1860—1911), Czech-born Austrian composer, wrote this letter to his wife, Alma, in 1910. Mahler was conductor at the Vienna State Opera and later the New York Philharmonic Society, as well as a composer of symphonies and songs.

The first rehearsal today. Went quite well and my physique held out quite gallantly. With every beat, I looked round and thought how lovely it would be if my divinity were seated down there and I could brush her dear face with a stolen glance — then I'd know what I was alive for and why I was doing it all.

...

Edith Wharton

Edith Wharton (1861—1937), American writer, wrote a series of loving letters to W. Morton Fullerton, an American journalist. She had been unhappily married. Fullerton, whom she met in Paris, was the one great love of her life, but soon faded out of it with a cruel lack of explanation. He later sold the love letters she had written to him. Any letters he may have sent to her have been lost. Born into a wealthy, aristocratic New York family, Wharton is best known for her novels, including *The House of Mirth* and *The Age of Innocence*, but she also wrote short stories, poetry, travel books and maintained a voluminous correspondence with her many friends, including Henry James. Below are some extracts from her correspondence with W. Morton Fullerton.

April 29th, 1910.

Send me a word today, Dear, to show your faith in *mine:* no matter how short, if it is clear & definite. If you tell me that at present we are not to see each other, I shall understand. My love for you is larger than all the pangs of vanity & jealousy!

The *not understanding* is the one unendurable and needless thing. All the rest, Dear, my heart has turned to beauty — & will one day turn to peace.

May 1910.

I said once that my life was better before I knew you. That is not so, for it is good to have lived once *in the round*, for ever so short a time. But my life *is* harder now because of those few months last summer, when I had my one glimpse of what a good camaraderie might be ... Before I knew you I had grown so impersonal, so accustomed to be my own only comrade, that even what I am going through now would have touched me less. When one is a lonely-hearted & remembering creature, as I am, it is a misfortune to love too late, & as completely as I have loved you. Everything else grows so ghostly afterward.

Isadora Duncan

Isadora Duncan (1878—1927), American dancer, conducted a romance with Gordon Craig, an English actor and stage designer, the son of the great actress Ellen Terry (herself the recipient of much fervent correspondence from George Bernard Shaw). The couple were intimate for several years, and had a child together. Duncan described her lover as 'the Wine & Poetry of Life'.

March 1907.

You send me poems that are caresses & words that are like kisses or a flock of little soft birds that fly down & nestle in and all about me & take away my senses. If you write me like that I will not wish to grow well but only to lie here with those delicious words nestling in my throat & my heart & singing me conscious only of Heaven. You cannot know what joy you give me — No you cannot know it — my heart is overflowing & I cannot write to you.

March 9th, 1907.

Someone knocked. My heart jumped up & down & I have your letter — only to touch it with my fingers & life comes rushing back to me — How sweet it is to hold your letter & to read it again & again. My whole being wakes up — it is like food to the starving.

...

Tsaritsa Alexandra

Tsaritsa Alexandra (1872—1918) was a German princess and Empress of Russia as the wife of Tsar Nicholas II, whom she married in 1894. The relationship between Alexandra and her husband was intensely affectionate, as their correspondence shows. She ruled the country during his absence at the front during the First World War and this letter, dated December 4th, 1916, was written during the time when he was often away with the Russian troops. When the revolution broke out the couple and their children were imprisoned by the Bolsheviks and executed in a cellar at Ekaterinberg in 1918.

My Very Precious One,
Good-bye, sweet Lovy!
It's great pain to let you go — worse than ever after the hard times we have been living & fighting through. But God who is all love & mercy has let the things take a change for the better ... just a little more patience and deepest faith in the prayers & help of our friend — then all will go well. I am fully convinced that great & beautiful times are coming for yr. reign & Russia. Only keep up your spirits, let no talks or letters pull you down — let them pass by as something unclean & quickly to be forgotten.

Show to all, that you are the Master & your will shall be obeyed — the time of great indulgence & gentleness is over — now comes your reign of will & power, & they shall be made to bow down before you & listen to your orders & work how & with whom you wish — obedience they must be taught, they do not know the meaning of that word, you have spoilt them by yr. kindness & all forgivingness …

But soon all this things will blow over its getting clearer & the weather too, which is a good sign, remember.

And our dear Friend is praying so hard for you — a man of God's near one gives the strength, faith & hope one needs so sorely. And others cannot understand this great calm of yours & therefore think you don't understand & try to ennervate, frighten & prick at you. But they will soon tire of it …

All is turning to the good — our Friends dreams mean so much. Sweetly, go to the *Moghilev* Virgin & find peace & strength there — look in after tea, before you receive, take Baby with you, quietly — its so calm there — & you can place yr. candels. Let the people see you are a christian Sovereign & don't be shy — even such an example will help others. —

How will the lonely nights be? I cannot imagine it. The consolation to hold you tightly clasped in my arms — it lulled the pain of soul & heart & I tried to put all my endless love, prayers & faith & strength into my caresses. So inexpressibly dear you are to me, husband of my heart. God bless you & my Baby treasure — I cover you with kisses; when sad, go to Baby's room & sit a bit quietly there with his nice people. Kiss the beloved child & you will feel warmed & calm. All my love I pour out to you, Sun of my life. —

Sleep well, heart & soul with you, my prayers around you — God & the holy Virgin will never forsake you —

Ever your very, very
Own

…

Franz Kafka

Franz Kafka (1883—1924), Czech-born Austrian writer, was twice engaged to marry Felice Bauer, but he broke off the relationship in the agonized belief that his ill-health and obsessiveness would not allow it to prosper. He wrote thousands of soul-baring letters to Felice between September 1912 and October 1917. The letters are extraordinary for their despairing though ironic self-knowledge. His will specified that none of these letters (or his diaries) should survive him but in fact it is Felice's side of the correspondence that has been lost. In March 1919, fifteen months after her final parting from Kafka, Felice married a well-to-do Berlin business man. The extracts below give a flavour of the correspondence.

October 31st, 1912.

When at last a letter arrives — after the door to my room has opened a thousand times to admit, not the man with the letter, but innumerable people whose calm expressions torment me because they feel themselves to be in the right place, whereas only the man with the letter, and no one else, has the right to appear — when at last the letter arrives, then I think for a while I can be calm, that I shall be satisfied by it and that the day will go well. But then I have read it, there is more in it than I might ever have expected to learn ... I read the letter once, put it aside, and read it again; I pick up a file but am really only reading your letter; I am with the typist, to whom I am supposed to dictate, and again your letter slowly slides through my fingers and I have begun to draw it out of my pocket when people ask me something and I know perfectly well I should not be thinking of your letter now, yet that thought is all that occurs to me — but after all that I am as hungry as before, as restless as before, and once again the door starts swinging merrily, as though the man with the letter were about to appear again. That is what you call the 'little pleasure' your letters give me.

November 14th, 1912.

Remember, you should sleep more than other people, for I sleep less, though not much less, than most. And I can't think of a better place to store my unused share of universal sleep than in your beloved eyes.

And no wild dreams, please! In my mind I am making a tour around your bed, demanding silence. And after I have put everything in order there, and perhaps even shooed away a drunk from the Immanuelkirchstrasse, I return, more orderly within myself as well, to my writing, or perhaps even straight to sleep.

November 24th, 1912.

With extreme cunning — and to distinguish myself by my cunning in the eyes of the beloved — I am sending each page of this Sunday letter (there are five) in a separate envelope on the assumption that the post office, though it seems to plague us, won't lose them all (even though it's Sunday, and they can't be registered). On the other hand, this method increases the risk of one page or another getting lost; well, I'm doing my best and will not invite danger by mentioning further fears.

December 23rd, 1912.

Dearest, my dearest, out of love for you, only out of love, I would like to dance with you; for I now feel that dancing, this embracing and turning at the same time, belongs inseparably to love and is its true and crazy expression.

February 17th—18th, 1913.

There are times, Felice, when I feel you have so much power over me that I think you could change me into a man capable of doing the obvious.

March 30th, 1913.

But then I simply cannot do without your letters. I am obsessed by the need for news of you. It is only through your letters that I become capable of even the most insignificant daily task. I need your letter to move my little finger properly.

October 29th, 1913.

My longing for you is such that it presses on my breast like tears that cannot be wept.

...

Alban Berg

Alban Berg (1885—1935), Austrian composer, married Helene Nahowski on August 3rd, 1911. His wife said of their relationship: 'For 28 years I lived in the Paradise of his love. His death was a catastrophe I only had the strength to survive because our souls were long ago joined together in a union beyond space and time, a union through all eternity.' His letters to her, some of which are extracted here, certainly bear this out.

Autumn 1907.

Truly, Helene, my dearest and most beloved, I found the splendour of yesterday's joy almost frightening. I have kissed you! I had to join my lips with yours, I was driven, irresistibly, by some inner force I would not escape. So much ecstasy all at once, my eyes were wet with tears, all my body and soul swamped in one great flood of emotion. This is how much I love you.

Dazed with delight, I staggered homewards, feeling only your sweet hand caressing my soul. I was rocked in bliss, bearing home on my lips the most glorious of kisses.

Spring 1909.

There is a delicate scent in my room. I have before me the second of your lovely veils, and when I press it to my face, I can almost feel the sweet warm breath from your mouth. The violets you picked for me yesterday, which nearly withered in my buttonhole, are now blooming anew, and smell soft and fresh. The cushion on the divan and the chair by the window belong to you, Helene, they have become appendages to your presence. Indeed everything in my room is the same: the mirror in front of which you arranged your hair; the window I have seen you looking through so seriously (even in our gayest moments); the last pale rays of sunlight which make your hair gleam with gold; the glowing fire in the stove; and then the laurel wreath, and the dear little cover on the bedside table — everything, everything is yours.

And that's no wonder seeing that I myself have become so entirely your 'creation'. All my possessions and even thoughts are somehow a loan or gift from *you*.

August 3rd, 1909.

Imagine one such day. In the early morning our nerves would be a-quiver as we rushed to meet each other — for the first kiss, the first embrace. Then into the forest, talking gaily or exchanging memories sweet or sad. The sun shines ever stronger, bringing quiet desire for the dark green waves of the lake. Then you come out of the cabin, with the sheen of your white body, the fragrance of your warm breath. We swim out into the waves, then back at last to the shore and our bath-robes. You lie with me in the grass and the sun's splendour; joy seeps through every pore of my body, that body which would wither without the power of your beauty. And another physical faculty, which I have long been without, would again emerge: my appetite! In the cool, sheltered veranda we should enjoy *Topfenhaluschka* or other simple dishes as if they were ambrosia. Then up into the quietness and peace of the cool room.

How short the rest of the day would seem, to taste everything our senses and nerves hanker after: music, singing, nature, exercise in the fresh air, drives, good books, fresh berries, boating, sunsets — all in a mad jumble to revel in at every chance. Then evening comes, the lanterns go out, and only the light of a candle shines here and there through the green shutters. All sounds of man and beast have subsided, and there seems only a single sound merging from the noises of the day, the chirping of the crickets, the continuous rippling of the wall outside the door. Then, when I open the door of your room, then, oh then, there would be nothing to part us any more. We should 'blissfully fall asleep in the arms of love'.

In the morning, long after the first cock-crow, as you rubbed your dear sleepy eyes, a last fond embrace would close the circle of happiness, of fulfilment: life's purpose attained.

Such a day would be worth the most miserable, tormented life; worth death itself.

...

Katherine Mansfield

Katherine Mansfield (1888—1923), New Zealand-born writer, and John Middleton Murry, English critic and writer, exchanged over 300 letters in their passionate (but not exclusive) eleven-year relationship, which ended with Mansfield's tragically early death from tuberculosis in 1923. They married in 1918 and worked together on literary magazines, but were often separated as Mansfield pursued warmth and sunshine in a futile attempt to escape her disease. After her death, Murry published Mansfield's poems, letters and a journal. Here is a small selection from her love letters to him.

March 27th, 1912.

Then I came in and read your Monday night letter — I read it and then I read it again — Then I dropped it into my heart and it made ever bigger circles of love — flowing over and over until I was quite healed of that torment of waiting. I love you — you know. I love you with every inch of me.

December 19th, 1915.

Writing to you I love you simply boundlessly. My love for you is always being new born; the heavenly dews descend upon it, and I'll not believe it is the same flower as yesterday — you see — how I believe in you! I have a store of belief in you that couldn't be exhausted! How I admire you! How I love you! — we are two little boys walking with our arms (which won't quite reach) round each other's shoulders and telling each other secrets and stopping to look at things ... We must not fail our love.

December 29th, 1915.

I have loved you before for 3 years with my heart and my mind but it seems to me that I have never loved you *avec mon âme* [with my soul] as I do now. I love you with all our future life — our life together which seems only now to have taken root and to be alive and growing up in the sun — *I* do not love you — but Love possesses me utterly love for you and for our life and for all our richness and joy. I have never felt anything like it before. In fact I did not comprehend the possibility of such a thing.

Vita Sackville-West

Vita Sackville-West (1892—1962), aristocratic English writer and gardener, wrote this tribute to her husband, Harold Nicolson, on 25th June, 1929.

You are dearer to me than anybody ever has been or ever could be. If you died suddenly, I should kill myself as soon as I had made provision for the boys. I really mean this. I could not live if I lost you. I do not think one could conceive of a love more exclusive, more tender, or more pure than I have for you. I think it is immortal, a thing which happens seldom.

Darling, there are not many people who would write such a letter after sixteen years of marriage, yet who would be saying therein only one-fiftieth of what they were feeling as they wrote it. I sometimes try to tell you the truth, and then I find that I have no words at my command which could possibly convey it to you.

...

Dylan Thomas

Dylan Thomas (1914—53), Welsh poet, wrote many love letters to his wife, Caitlin. They were married in 1937. She was the mistress of the painter Augustus John when they met. The marriage was always stormy. Thomas died after a drinking binge in New York in 1953.

Late 1936.

I love you so much I'll never be able to tell you; I'm frightened to tell you. I can always feel your heart. Dance tunes are always right: I love you body and soul: — and I suppose body means that I want to touch you & be in bed with you, & I suppose soul means that I can hear you & see you & love you in every single, single thing in the whole world asleep or awake.

June 24th, 1945.

You are the most beautiful girl that has ever lived, and it is worth dying to have kissed you.

March 11th, 1950.

Caitlin my own own own dearest love whom God and *my* love and your love for me protect, my sweet wife, my dear one, my Irish heart, my wonderful wonderful girl who is with me invisibly every second of these dreadful days, awake or sleepless, who is forever and forever with me and is my own true beloved amen — I love you,

67

I need you, I want, want you, we have never been apart as long as this, never, never, and we will never be again. I am writing to you now, lying in bed, in the Roman Princess's sister's rich social house, in a posh room that is hell on earth. Oh why, why, *didn't* we arrange it *somehow* that we came out together to this devastating, insane, demoniacally loud, roaring continent. We *could* somehow have arranged it. Why oh why did I think I could live, I could bear to live, I could think of living, for all these torturing, unending, echoing months without you, Cat, my life, my wife, my wife on earth and in God's eyes, my reason for my blood, breath, and bone. Here, in this vast, mad horror, that doesn't know its size, or its strength, or its weakness, or its barbaric speed, stupidity, din, selfrighteousness, this cancerous Babylon, here we could cling together, sane, safe, & warm & face, together, everything. I LOVE YOU.

May 7th, 1950.

Darling darling dear my dear Caitlin, oh God how I love you, oh God how far away you are, I love you night, day, every second, every oceanic deep second of time, of life, of sense, of love, of any meaning at all, that is spent away from you and in which I only think of coming back, coming back, to you, my heart, my sacred sweetheart, Caitlin my dear one.

...

Sylvia Plath

Sylvia Plath (1932—63), American poet, wrote this celebration of love to her mother, Aurelia Schober Plath, on October 8th, 1956. Plath, a brilliant and ambitious writer, had a history of depression and her fragile mental state is evident in many of the thousand letters she wrote to her mother. She attempted to take her own life more than once and finally succeeded in February 1963, following the breakdown of her 1956 marriage to the English poet Ted Hughes.

In the course of this working and vital summer, we have mystically become one. I can appreciate the legend of Eve coming from Adam's rib as I never did before; the damn story's true! That's where I belong. Away from Ted, I feel as if I were living with one eyelash of myself only. It is really agony. We *are* different from most couples; for we share ourselves perhaps more intensely at every moment. Everything I do with and for Ted has a celestial radiance ... I need no sorrow to write; I have had, and, no doubt, will have enough. My poems and stories I want to be the strongest female paean yet for the creative forces of nature, the joy of being a loved and loving woman; that is my song.

Family Life
&
Friends

Love is the life of friendship:
letters are the life of love.

James Howell (1593—1666)
Welsh writer

Agrippina

Agrippina (c. 15—59 AD), wife of the Emperor Claudius, wrote this letter to her son, Nero, in effect pleading for her life. Her son and his mistress, Poppaea Sabina, had concocted treason charges against her. Her pleas fell on deaf ears; Nero had her strangled to death.

Don't you know, my son, the affection all mothers naturally bear their children? Our love is unbounded, incessantly fed by that tenderness unknown to all but ourselves. Nothing should be more dear to us than what we have bought with the risk of our lives; nothing more precious than what we have endured such grief and pain to procure. These are so acute and unbearable that if it were not for the vision of a successful birth, which makes us forget our agonies, generation would soon cease.

Do you forget that nine full months I carried you in my womb and nourished you with my blood? How likely is it, then, that I would destroy the dear child who cost me so much anguish to bring into the world? It may be that the just gods were angry at my excessive love of you, and used this way to punish me.

Unhappy Agrippina! You are suspected of a crime of which nobody could really think you guilty ... What does the title of empress mean to me, if I am accused of a crime that even the basest of women would abhor? Unhappy are those who breathe the air of the court. The wisest of people are not secure from storms in that harbour. There even a calm is dangerous.

...

Sir Walter Raleigh

Sir Walter Raleigh (1552—1618), English courtier and explorer, wrote this tender farewell to his wife, Bess, in 1603. Once a favourite of Queen Elizabeth I, his enemies had him brought to trial on charges of conspiracy against the Crown. He wrote this letter from the Tower of London, but in fact he was not executed the next day as he expected; after a reprieve in which he was allowed to undertake an expedition in South America, he was rearrested and finally executed in 1618.

You shall now receive (my deare wife) my last words in these my last lines. My love I send you that you may keep it when I am dead, and my councell that you may remember it when I am no more. I would not by my will present you with sorrowes (dear Besse) let them go to the grave with me and be buried in the dust. And seeing that it is not Gods will that I should see you any more in this life, beare it patiently, and with a heart like thy selfe.

First, I send you all the thankes which my heart can conceive, or my words can rehearse for your many travailes, and care taken for me, which though they have not taken effect as you wished, yet my debt to you is not the lesse: but pay it I never shall in this world.

Secondly, I beseech you for the love you beare me living, do not hide your selfe many dayes, but by your travailes seeke to helpe your miserable fortunes and the right of your poor childe. Thy mourning cannot availe me, I am but dust ...

Love God and begin betimes to repose your selfe upon him, and therein shall you finde true and lasting riches, and endlesse comfort: for the rest when you have travailed and wearied your thoughts over all sorts of worldly cogitations, you shall but sit downe by sorrowe in the end ...

My deare wife farewell. Blesse my poore boy. Pray for me, and let my good God hold you both in his armes.

Written with the dying hand of sometimes thy Husband, but now alasse overthrowne.

Yours that was, but now my own.

...

Madame Marie de Sévigné

Madame Marie de Sévigné (1626—96), French woman of letters, wrote a fascinating series of letters to her daughter, Madame de Grignan, whom she loved dotingly. Their separations caused de Sévigné endless distress. She left to return to Paris on the day this letter was written, October 5th, 1673, while her daughter went on a journey to Salons and Aix.

This is a dreadful day, my dear child; I own I can scarcely support it. I have left you in a situation that adds to my sorrow. I think of every step I take, and every one you take; and that were we to continue travelling in this way, we should never meet again ... My heart and mind are full of you; I cannot think of you without weeping, and I think of you incessantly. This state is not to be borne: as it is extreme, I hope its violence will destroy it. I seek you continually, and I seem to have lost everything in losing you. My eyes, that have so often for these fourteen months dwelt on you with delight, no longer behold you; the endearing time I have passed, renders the present more painful, till I am a little accustomed to it, but I shall never be sufficiently accustomed to it not to desire ardently to see and embrace you again. I have no reason to hope more from the future than the past. I know what I have already suffered by your absence; and I shall now be still more to be pitied, since I have imprudently made your presence necessary to me ...

I already begin to be devoured with expectation. I hope for no consolation but from your letters; and yet I know they will only make me sigh still more deeply. In short, my dear child, I live but for you. Would I loved God with equal fervour!

...

Jonathan Swift

Jonathan Swift (1667—1745), Irish writer, enjoyed an epistolary friendship with the English writer Alexander Pope. Swift was the Dean of St Patrick's Cathedral in Dublin as well as a poet and satirist. His world-famous satire, *Gulliver's Travels*, was published in 1726. This letter was written on February 7th, 1735 or 1736.

It is some time since I dined at the Bishop of Derry's, where Mr Secretary Cary told me with great concern that you were taken very ill. I have heard nothing since; only I have continued in great pain of mind; yet for my own sake and the world's more than for yours; because I well know how little you value life both as a philosopher and a Christian, particularly the latter, wherein hardly one in a million of us heretics can equal you.

If you are well recovered, you ought to be reproached for not putting me especially out of pain, who could not bear the loss of you; although we must be for ever distant as much as if I were in the grave, for which my years and continual indisposition are preparing me every season. I have staid too long from pressing you to give me some ease by an account of your health ...

I have nobody now left but you. Pray be so kind to outlive me; and then die as soon as you please; but without pain; and let us meet in a better place, if my religion will permit, but rather my virtue, although much unequal to yours ... My state of health is not to boast of; my giddiness is more or less too constant; I sleep ill, and have a poor appetite. I can as easily write a poem in the Chinese language as my own. I am as fit for matrimony as invention; and yet I have daily schemes for innumerable essays in prose, and proceed sometimes to no less than half a dozen lines, which the next morning become waste paper. What vexes me most is, that my female friends, who could bear me very well a dozen years ago, have now forsaken me; although I am not so old in proportion to them as I formerly was: which I can prove by arithmetic, for then I was double their age, which now I am not.

...

The Fourth Earl of Chesterfield

Philip Dormer Stanhope (1694—1773), fourth Earl of Chesterfield, English diplomat and statesman, wrote a famous series of letters to his illegitimate son. The boy was the product of an affair with a French governess while Chesterfield was ambassador to The Hague. The two men were not close — Chesterfield was not even informed of his son's marriage to the greedy Eugenia, who published his letters, not intended for publication, while he was still alive. This letter is dated March 6th, 1747.

Whatever you do, will always affect me, very sensibly, one way or another; and I am now most agreeably affected by two letters, which I have lately seen from Lausanne, upon your subject ... they both give so good an account of you ... They write, that you are not only *décrotté*, but tolerably well-bred; and that the English crust of awkward bashfulness, shyness and roughness ... is pretty well rubbed off. I am most heartily glad of it; for, as I have often told you, those lesser talents, of an engaging, insinuating manner, an easy good-breeding, a genteel behaviour and address, are of infinitely more advantage than they are generally thought to be, especially here in England.

Virtue and learning, like gold, have their intrinsic value; but if they are not polished, they certainly lose a great deal of their lustre: and even polished brass will pass upon more people than rough gold.

What a number of sins does the cheerful, easy good-breeding of the French frequently cover! Many of them want common sense, many more common learning; but, in general, they make up so much, by their manner, for those defects, that, frequently, they pass undiscovered ...

You know what virtue is: you may have it if you will; it is in every man's power; and miserable is the man who has it not. Good-sense God has given you. Learning you already possess enough of, to have, in a reasonable time, all that a man need have. With this, you are thrown out early into the world, where it will be your own fault if you do not acquire all the other accomplishments necessary to complete and adorn your character.

...

Fanny Burney

Fanny Burney (1752—1840), English novelist, wrote this harrowing account of her mastectomy in a letter to her sister, Esther, in 1812. She had been diagnosed as having cancer in her right breast the previous year. Burney's letters and diaries provide valuable insights into life at court and in France, where she lived with her husband General Alexandre d'Arblay from 1802 until 1811.

A formal consultation now was held, of Larrey, Ribe, & Moreau — &, in fine, I was formally condemned to an operation by all Three. I was as much astonished as disappointed — for the poor breast was no where discoloured, & not much larger than its healthy neighbour. Yet I felt the evil to be deep, so deep, that I often thought if it could not be dissolved, it could only with life be extirpated. I called up, however, all the reason I possessed, or could assume, & told them — that if they saw no other alternative, I would not resist their opinion & experience: — the good Dr Larrey, who, during his long attendance had conceived for me the warmest friendship, had now tears in his Eyes ...

My heart beat fast: I saw all hope was over. I called upon them to speak. M. Dubois then, after a long & unintelligible harangue, from his own disturbance, pronounced my doom. I now saw it was inevitable, and abstained from any further effort. They received my formal consent, & retired to fix a day.

All hope of escaping this evil being now at an end, I could only console or employ my mind in considering how to render it less dreadful to M. d'A. M. Dubois had pronounced 'il faut s'attendre à souffrir, Je ne veux pas vous trompez — Vous Souffrirez — vous souffrirez *beaucoup*! —' M. Ribe had *charged* me to cry! to withhold or restrain myself might have seriously bad consequences, he said. M. Moreau, in ecchoing this injunction, enquired whether I had cried or screamed at the birth of Alexander — Alas, I told him, it had not been possible to do otherwise; Oh then, he answered, there is no fear! — What terrible inferences were here to be drawn! I desired, therefore, that M. d'A. might be kept in ignorance of the day till the operation should be over. To this they agreed, except M. Larrey, with high approbation: M. Larrey looked dissentient, but was silent. M. Dubois protested he would not undertake to act, after what he had seen of the agitated spirits of M. d'A. if he were present: nor would he suffer me to know the time myself over night; I obtained with difficulty a promise of 4 hours warning, which were essential to me for sundry regulations.

From this time, I assumed the best spirits in my power, *to meet the coming blow*; — & support my too sympathising Partner. They would let me make no preparations, refusing to inform me what would be necessary ...

After sentence thus passed, I was in hourly expectation of a summons to execution; judge, then, my surprise to be suffered to go on full 3 Weeks in the same state! M. Larrey from time to time visited me, but pronounced nothing, & was always melancholy. At length, M. d'A. was told that he waited himself for a Summons! & that, a formal one, & in writing! I could not give one, a *consent* was my utmost effort. But poor M. d'A. wrote a desire that the operation, if necessary, might take place without further delay. In my own mind, I had all this time been persuaded there were hopes of a cure: why else, I thought, let me know my doom thus long? But here I must account for this apparently useless, & therefore cruel measure, though I only learnt it myself 2 months afterwards. M. Dubois had given his opinion that the evil was too far advanced for any remedy; that the cancer was already internally declared; that I was inevitably destined to that most frightful of deaths, & that an operation would but accellerate my dissolution. Poor M. Larrey was so deeply affected by this sentence, that — as he has lately told me, — he regretted to his Soul ever having known me, & was upon the point of demanding a commission to the furthest end of France in order to force me into other hands. I had said, however, he remembered, once, that I would far rather suffer a quick end without, than a lingering life with this dreadfullest of maladies: he finally, therefore, considered it might be possible to save me by the trial, but that without it my case was desperate, & resolved to make the attempt. Nevertheless, the responsibility was too great to rest upon his own head entirely; & therefore he waited the formal summons. — In fine, One morning — the last of September, 1811 ... another Letter was delivered to me — another, indeed! — 'twas from M. Larrey, to acquaint me that at 10 o'clock he should be with me, properly accompanied, & to exhort me to rely as much upon his sensibility & his prudence, as upon his dexterity & his experience; he charged to secure the absence of M. d'A: & told me that the young Physician who would deliver me this *announce*, would prepare for the operation, in which he must lend his aid: & also that it had been the decision of the consultation to allow me but two hours notice ...

This indeed, was a dreadful interval. I had no longer any thing to do — I had only to think — TWO HOURS thus spent seemed never-ending. I would fain have written to my dearest Father — to You, my Esther — to Charlotte James   Charles — Amelia Lock — but my arm prohibited me: I strolled to the Sallon — I saw it fitted with preparations, & I recoiled — But I soon returned; to what effect disguise from myself what I must so soon know? — yet the sight of the immense quantity of bandages, compresses, spunges, Lint — made me a little sick: — I walked backwards & forwards till I quieted all emotion, & became, by degrees, nearly stupid — torpid, without sentiment or consciousness; — & thus I remained till the Clock struck three. A sudden spirit of exertion then returned, — I defied my poor arm, no longer worth sparing, & took my long banished pen to write a few words to M. d'A — & a few more for Alex, in case of a fatal result. These short billets I could only deposit safely, when the Cabriolets — one — two — three — four — succeeded rapidly to each other in stopping at the door. Dr Moreau

75

instantly entered my room, to see if I were alive. He gave me a wine cordial, & went to the Sallon. I rang for my Maid & Nurses, — but before I could speak to them, my room, without previous message, was entered by 7 men in black, Dr Larry, M. Dubois, Dr Moreau, Dr Aumont, Dr Ribe, & a pupil of Dr Larry, & another of M. Dubois. I was now awakened from my stupor — & by a sort of indignation — Why so many? & without leave? — But I could not utter a syllable. M. Dubois acted as Commander in Chief. Dr Larry kept out of sight; M. Dubois ordered a Bed stead into the middle of the room. Astonished, I turned to Dr Larry, who had promised that an Arm Chair would suffice; but he hung his head, & would not look at me. *Two old mattresses* M. Dubois then demanded, & an old Sheet. I now began to tremble violently, more with distaste & horrour of the preparations even than of the pain. These arranged to his liking, he desired me to mount the Bed stead. I stood suspended, for a moment, whether I should not abruptly escape — I looked at the door, the windows — I felt desperate — but it was only for a moment, my reason then took the command, & my fears & feelings struggled vainly against it. I called to my maid — she was crying, & the two Nurses stood, transfixed, at the door. Let those women all go! cried M. Dubois. This order recovered me my Voice — No, I cried, let them stay! *qu'elles restent!* …

M. Dubois placed me upon the mattress, & spread a cambric handkerchief upon my face. It was transparent, however, & I saw, through it, that the Bed stead was instantly surrounded by the 7 men & my nurse. I refused to be held; but when, Bright through the cambric, I saw the glitter of polished Steel — I closed my Eyes. I would not trust to convulsive fear the sight of the terrible incision. A silence the most profound ensued, which lasted for some minutes, during which, I imagine, they took their orders by signs, & made their examination — Oh what a horrible suspension! — I did not breathe — & M. Dubois tried vainly to find any pulse. This pause, at length, was broken by Dr Larry, who, in a voice of solemn melancholy, said 'Qui me tiendra ce sein?—'

No one answered; at least not verbally; but this aroused me from my passively submissive state, for I feared they imagined the whole breast infected — feared it too justly, — for, again through the Cambric, I saw the hand of M. Dubois held up, while his fore finger first described a straight line from top to bottom of the breast, secondly a Cross, & thirdly a Circle; intimating that the WHOLE was to be taken off. Excited by this idea, I started up, threw off my veil, &, in answer to the demand 'Qui me tiendra ce sein?', cried 'C'est moi, Monsieur!' & I held my hand under it, & I explained the nature of my sufferings, which all sprang from one point, though they darted into every part. I was heard attentively, but in utter silence, & M. Dubois then re-placed me as before, &, as before, spread my veil over my face. How vain, alas, my representation! immediately again I saw the fatal finger describe the Cross — & the circle — Hopeless, then, desperate, & self-given up, I closed once more my Eyes, relinquishing all watching, all resistance, all interference, & sadly resolute to be wholly resigned.

My dearest Esther, — & all my dears to whom she communicates this doleful ditty, will rejoice to hear that this resolution once taken, was firmly adhered to, in defiance of a terror that surpasses all description, & the most torturing pain. Yet — when the dreadful steel was plunged into the breast — cutting through veins — arteries — flesh — nerves — I needed no injunctions not to restrain my cries. I began a scream that lasted unintermittingly during the whole time of the incision — & I almost marvel that it rings not in my Ears still! so excruciating was the agony. When the wound was made, & the instrument was withdrawn, the pain seemed undiminished, for the air that suddenly rushed into those delicate parts felt like a mass of minute but sharp & forked poniards, that were tearing the edges of the wound — but when again I felt the instrument — describing a curve — cutting against the grain, if I may so say, while the flesh resisted in a manner so forcible as to oppose & tire the hand of the operator, who was forced to change from the right to the left — then, indeed, I thought I must have expired. I attempted no more to open my Eyes, — they felt as if hermettically shut, & so firmly closed, that the Eyelids seemed indented into the Cheeks. The instrument this second time withdrawn, I concluded the operation over — Oh no! presently the terrible cutting was renewed — & worse than ever, to separate the bottom, the foundation of this dreadful gland from the parts to which it adhered — Again all description would be baffled — yet again all was not over, — Dr Larry rested but his own hand, & — Oh Heaven! — I then felt the Knife [rack]ling against the breast bone — scraping it! — This performed, while I yet remained in utterly speechless torture, I heard the Voice of Mr Larry, — (all others guarded a dead silence) in a tone nearly tragic, desire every one present to pronounce if any thing more remained to be done; The general voice was Yes, — but the finger of Mr Dubois — which I literally *felt* elevated over the wound, though I saw nothing, & though he touched nothing, so indescribably sensitive was the spot — pointed to some further requisition — & again began the scraping! — and, after this, Dr Moreau thought he discerned a peccant attom — and still, & still, M. Dubois demanded attom after attom — My dearest Esther, not for days, not for Weeks, but for Months I could not speak of this terrible business without nearly again going through it! I could not *think* of it with impunity! I was sick, I was disordered by a single question — even now, 9 months after it is over, I have a head ache from going on with the account! & this miserable account, which I began 3 Months ago, at least, I dare not revise, nor read, the recollection is still so painful.

To conclude, the evil was so profound, the case so delicate, & the precautions necessary for preventing a return so numerous, that the operation, including the treatment & the dressing, lasted 20 minutes! a time, for sufferings so acute, that was hardly supportable — However, I bore it with all the courage I could exert, & never moved, nor stopt them, nor resisted, nor remonstrated, nor spoke — except once or twice, during the dressings, to say 'Ah Messieurs! que je vous plains! —' for indeed I was sensible to the feeling concern with which they all saw what I endured, though my speech was principally — *very* principally meant for Dr Larry. Except this, I uttered not a syllable, save, when so often they recommenced, calling out 'Avertissez moi, Messieurs avertissez moi!—' Twice, I believe, I fainted; at least, I have two total chasms in my memory of this transaction, that impede my tying together what passed. When all was done, & they lifted me up that I might be put to bed, my strength was so totally annihilated, that I was obliged to be carried, & could not even sustain my hands & arms, which hung as if I had been lifeless; while my face, as the Nurse has told me, was utterly colourless. This removal made me open my Eyes — & I then saw my good Dr Larry, pale nearly as myself, his face streaked with blood, & its expression depicting grief, apprehension, & almost horrour.

...

William Wordsworth

William Wordsworth (1770—1850) wrote this grim account to fellow English poet Robert Southey on December 2nd, 1812. Wordsworth's son, Thomas, was six years old when he died.

Symptoms of the measles appeared upon my Son Thomas last Thursday; he was most favorable held till tuesday, between ten and eleven at that hour was particularly lightsome and comfortable; without any assignable cause a sudden change took place, an inflammation had commenced on the lungs which it was impossible to check and the sweet Innocent yielded up his soul to God before six in the evening ... My Wife bears the loss of her Child with striking fortitude ... For myself dear Southey I dare not say in what state of mind I am; I loved the Boy with the utmost love of which my soul is capable, and he is taken from me — yet in the agony of my spirit in surrendering such a treasure I feel a thousand times richer than if I had never possessed it. God comfort and save you and all our friends and us all from a repetition of such trials — O Southey feel for me!

...

Jane Austen

Jane Austen (1775—1850), English novelist, was extremely close to her sister, Cassandra. The vivid letters to Cassandra have given the world the best insight into Jane Austen's private life. However, this letter to her niece, Fanny Knight, also gives a wonderful view of Austen's vivacity and sense of humour. It is dated February 20th—21st, 1817.

My dearest Fanny,

You are inimitable, irresistable. You are the delight of my Life. Such Letters, such entertaining Letters as you have lately sent! — Such a description of your queer little heart! — Such a lovely display of what Imagination does. — You are worth your weight in Gold, or even in the new Silver Coinage. — I cannot express to you what I have felt in reading your history of yourself, how full of Pity & Concern & Admiration & Amusement I have been. You are the Paragon of all that is Silly & Sensible, common-place & eccentric, Sad & Lively, Provoking & Interesting. — Who can keep pace with the fluctuations of your Fancy, the Capprizios of your Taste, the Contradictions of your Feelings? — You are so odd! — & all the time, so perfectly natural — so peculiar in yourself, & yet so like everybody else! — It is very, very gratifying to me to know you so intimately. You can hardly think what a pleasure it is to me, to have such thorough pictures of your Heart. — Oh! what a loss it will be, when you are married. You are too agreable in your single state, too agreable as a Neice. I shall hate you when your delicious play of Mind is all settled down into conjugal & maternal affections. Mr. J. W. frightens me. — He will have you. — I see you at the Altar. — I have *some* faith in Mrs C. Cage's observation, & still more in Lizzy's; & besides, I know it *must* be so. He must be wishing to attach you. It would be too stupid & too shameful in him, to be otherwise; & all the Family are seeking your acquaintance. — Do not imagine that I have any real objection, I have rather taken a fancy to him than not, & I like Chilham Castle for you; — I only do not like you shd marry anybody. And yet I do wish you to marry very much, because I know you will never be happy till you are; but the loss of a Fanny Knight will be never made up to me; My 'affec: Neice F. C. Wildman' will be but a poor Substitute. I do not like your being nervous & so apt to cry; — it is a sign you are not quite well, but I hope Mr Scud — as you always write his name, (your Mr *Scuds*: amuse me very much) will do you good. — What a comfort that Cassandra should be so recovered! — It is more than we had expected. — I can easily beleive she was very patient & very good. I always loved Cassandra, for her fine dark eyes & sweet temper. — I am almost entirely cured of my rheumatism; just a little pain in my knee now & then, to make me remember what it was, & keep on flannel. — Aunt Cassandra nursed me so beautifully! — I enjoy your visit to Goodnestone, it must be a great pleasure to you, You have not seen Fanny Cage in any comfort so long. I hope she represents & remonstrates & reasons with you, properly. Why should you be living in dread of his marrying somebody else? — (Yet, how natural!) — You did not chuse to have him yourself; why not allow him to take comfort where he can? — In your conscience you *know* that he could not bear a comparison with a more animated Character. — You cannot forget how you felt under the idea of its having been possible that he might have dined in Hans Place. — My dearest Fanny, I cannot bear You should be unhappy about him. Think of his Principles, think of his Father's objection, of want of Money, of a coarse Mother, of Brothers & Sisters like Horses, of Sheets sewn across &c. — But I am doing no good — no, all that I urge against him will rather make you take his part more, sweet perverse Fanny. — And now I will tell you that we like your Henry to the utmost, to the very top of the Glass, quite brimful. — He is a very pleasing young Man. I do not see how he could be mended. He does really bid fair to be every thing his Father & Sister could wish; and William I love very much indeed, & so we do all, he is quite our own William. In short we are very comfortable together — that is, we can answer for *ourselves*. — Mrs Deedes is as welcome as May, to all our Benevolence to her Son; we only lamented that we cd not do more, & that the £50 note we slipt into his hand at parting was necessarily the Limit of our Offering. — Good Mrs Deedes! — I hope she will get the better of this Marianne, & then I wd recommend to her & Mr D. the simple regimen of separate rooms. — Scandal & Gossip; — yes I dare say you are well stocked; but I am very fond of Mrs C. Cage, for reasons good. Thank you for mentioning her praise of *Emma* &c. — I have contributed the marking to Uncle H.'s shirts, & now they are a complete memorial of the tender regard of many. — *Friday*. I had no idea when I began this yesterday, of sending it before your Br went back, but I have written away my foolish thoughts at such a rate that I will not keep them many hours longer to stare me in the face. — Much obliged for the *Quadrilles*, which I am grown to think pretty enough, though of course they are very inferior to the Cotillions of my own day. — Ben & Anna walked here last Sunday to hear Uncle Henry, & she looked so pretty, it was quite a pleasure to see her, so young & so blooming & so innocent, as if she had never had a wicked Thought in her Life — which yet one has some reason to suppose she must have had, if we beleive the Doctrine of Original Sin, or if we remember the events of her girlish days. — I hope Lizzy will have her Play. Very kindly arranged for her. Henry is generally thought very good-looking but not so handsome as Edward. — I think I prefer his face. — Wm is in excellent Looks, has a fine appetite & seems perfectly well. — You will have a great Break-up at Gm in the Spring, You *must* feel their all going. It is very right however. One sees many good causes for it. — Poor Miss C. — I shall pity her, when she begins to understand herself. — Your objection to the Quadrilles delighted me exceedingly. — Pretty Well, for a Lady irrecoverably attached to *one* Person! — Sweet Fanny, beleive no such thing of yourself. — Spread no such malicious slander upon your Understanding, within the Precincts of your Imagination. — Do not speak ill of your Sense, merely for the Gratification of your Fancy. — Yours is Sense, which deserves more honourable Treatment. — You are *not* in love with him. You never have been really in love with him. — Yrs very affecly

J. Austen

Note: Cassandra Austen wrote to Fanny Knight on the death of Jane, on July 20th, 1817.

I *have* lost a treasure, such a Sister, such a friend as never can have been surpassed, — She was the sun of my life, the gilder of every pleasure, the soother of every sorrow, I had not a thought concealed from her, & it is as if I had lost a part of myself.

...

George Gordon, Lord Byron

George Gordon, Lord Byron (1788—1824), English poet, fell in love with his half-sister, Augusta Leigh, and fathered a daughter with her. The resultant scandal probably destroyed his subsequent marriage, and was one of the reasons for which he fled England forever in 1816. This letter was written on March 22nd, 1804, when Byron and his half-sister were beginning to get to know each other after childhood separation.

Although, My ever Dear Augusta, I have hitherto appeared remiss in replying to your kind and affectionate letters; yet I hope you will not attribute my neglect to a want of affection, but rather to a shyness naturally inherent in my Disposition. I will now endeavour as amply as lies in my power to repay your kindness, and for the Future I hope you will consider me not only as *a Brother* but as your warmest and most affectionate *Friend*, and if ever Circumstances should require it as your *protector*. Recollect, My Dearest Sister, that you are *the nearest relation* I have in *the world both by the ties of Blood* and *Affection*. If there is anything in which I can serve you; you have only to mention it; Trust to your Brother, and be assured he will never betray your confidence ... Write to me Soon, my Dear Augusta, And do not forget to love me, In the meantime I remain more than words [can] express, your ever sincere, affectionate,
　　Brother and Friend
　　Byron

...

John Keats

John Keats (1795—1821), English poet, wrote this letter of comfort to his brother and sister-in-law, George and Georgiana Keats, in October 1818. Fanny was Keats's sister, and Tom, his younger brother who was dying of consumption.

Ours are ties which independent of their own Sentiment are sent us by providence to prevent the deleterious effects of one great, solitary grief. I have Fanny and I have you — three people whose Happiness to me is sacred — and it does not annul that selfish sorrow which I should otherwise fall into, living as I do with poor Tom who looks upon me as his only comfort — the tears will come into your Eyes — let them — and embrace each other ... Your content in each other is a delight to me which I cannot express ...

...

Mary Shelley

Mary Shelley (1797—1851), English writer, kept up a lively correspondence with many literary figures of her time. She was a prolific writer of fiction, including the classic Gothic novel *Frankenstein*, travel books, dramas, essays, reviews and poems. Her life was plagued by misfortune and poverty. Only one of her three adored children survived childhood, and her husband, the poet Percy Bysshe Shelley, was drowned in a boating accident at the age of 30. Here are some selections from her correspondence.

To Marianne Hunt, wife of the poet Leigh Hunt, June 29th, 1819.

You see by our hap how blind we mortals are when we go seeking after what we think our good — We came to Italy thinking to do Shelley's health good — but the Climate is not any means warm enough to be of benefit to him & yet it is that that has destroyed my two children — We went from England comparatively prosperous & happy — I should return broken hearted & miserable — I never know one moments ease from the wretchedness & despair that possesses me — May you my dear Marianne never know what it is to lose two only & lovely children in one year — to watch their dying moments — & then at last to be left childless and for ever miserable.

To her friend, Maria Gisborne, on the death of Shelley, August 27th, 1822.

God knows what will become of me! My life is now very monotonous as to outward events — yet how diversified by internal feeling – How often in the intensity of grief does one instant seem to fill & embrace the universe ... Solitude is my only help & resource; accustomed even when he was with me to spend much of my time alone, I can at those moments forget myself — until some idea, which I think I would communicate to him, occurs & then the yawning & dark gulph again displays itself unshaded by the rainbows which the imagination had formed. Despair, energy, love, despondency & excessive affliction are like clouds, driven across my mind, one by one, until tears blot the scene, & weariness of spirit consigns me to temporary repose.

To Jane Williams, whose husband Edward died in the same boating accident as Percy Bysshe Shelley, January 12th, 1823. Jane Williams was, for a time, Mary Shelley's closest friend and confidante, but Williams later deeply disappointed Shelley by spreading malicious tales about her and thereby deprived her of a trusted companion and emotional support. In 1827 Jane Williams was re-married to Thomas Jefferson Hogg.

Come to Florence, my dear Jane, & let us see if mutual affection will not stand us in some stead in our calamities — Our fate is one, so ought our interests here to be; we can talk eternally to each other of our lost ones, and surely they would be best pleased to find us together. I will deserve your love — if love can buy its like; and with me — perhaps you may attain the peaceful state you desire — I might ease you of some of your cares — & your affection to me would be a treasure.

...

Marjory Fleming

Marjory Fleming (1803—11), a brilliant young Scottish girl, died from the measles aged eight. During her short life she produced copious journals, letters and verses. She frequently refers to 'Isabella', which was the name shared by her mother, her elder sister, her cousin and a friend. The Isabella in this extract is probably her older cousin, tutor and playmate, Isabella Keith.

I confess that I have been more like a little young Devil then a creature for when Isabella went up the stairs to teach me religion and my multiplication and to be good and all my other lessons I stamped with my feet and threw my new hat which she made on the ground and was sulky an was dreadfully pasionate but she never whipped me but gently said Marjory go into another room and think what a great crime you are committing letting your temper git the better of you ...

...

George Sand

George Sand (Amantine Aurore Dudevant) (1804—76), French writer, became an intimate friend of the French historian, Countess Marie d'Agoult. George Sand scandalized French society with her unconventional ways and love affairs with the composer Chopin and the writer de Musset, among others. After her legal separation from her husband, Baron Casimir Dudevant, she permanently adopted the name George Sand, under which all her many works — novels, plays and letters — were published. This letter to d'Agoult is dated November 1st, 1835.

Friendship is too serious and too overruling a matter for me. If you wish me to love you, you must therefore begin by loving me; that is quite right, I will prove it to you. A soft and white hand meets the lovely back of a porcupine. The charming animal is fully aware that the white hand will not do him any harm. He knows that he, poor wretch, is scarcely inviting enough to be made a pet of. Before returning the caresses bestowed upon him, he waits until the hand has grown accustomed to his pricks; for, if the hand he loves shrinks from him (there is no reason why it should not), although the porcupine may exclaim, 'It is not my fault', that will not at all console him.

Consider then whether you can give your heart to a porcupine. I am capable of anything. I will play a thousand silly tricks; I will tread upon your toes; I will make rude replies without the least provocation; I will reproach you with a defect which you do not possess; I will suspect you of an intention which you never had; I will turn my back upon you; in short, I will make myself unbearable, until I am quite sure that I cannot make you cross and disgust you with me.

I will then carry you upon my back; I will do your cooking; I will wash your plates; all you will say will sound divine to me. If you happen to tread on some dirt, I will think it smells nice. I will see you with the same eyes that I have for myself when I am well and of a cheerful humour; that is to say that I consider myself as perfection, and all that is not of my way of thinking the object of my deep contempt. Do, then, your best that you may enter my eyes, my ears, my veins, my whole being. You will, in that case, learn that nobody on earth loves more than I, because I love without being ashamed of the reason why I love. That reason is the gratitude I feel towards those who adopt me. That is my summing up. It is not modest, but it is sincere.

...

Felix Mendelssohn-Bartholdy

Felix Mendelssohn-Bartholdy (1809—47), German composer, wrote this amusing letter to his family on April 25th, 1829. Mendelssohn travelled extensively during his lifetime, and was particularly fond of England. He was born into a wealthy, cultured family, and, unlike many other musicians, never had to worry about earning a living.

It is terrible! It is crazy! I am dazed and my head is spinning! London is the grandest and most complicated monstrosity on the face of the earth. How can I pack into a single letter all I have been through in the last three days? ... Such confusion! Such a maelstrom! I ask nothing better than to become historical and describe it all calmly, else you will make nothing of it; but if you only could see me, sitting near the heavenly grand piano that Clementi have just sent along for the duration of my stay, beside a cheerful fire, within my own four walls ... my breakfast tea and dry toast still in front of me, the servant-girl, with her hair in curl-papers, just bringing me my new cravat and asking for my orders — at which I try to nod in the polite English manner jerking my head backwards — and the fashionable, fog-shrouded street; and if you could only hear the pitiful tones of the beggar who has just struck up a song under my window ... and if you but knew that from here to the City is a three-quarter hour drive and that all the way along, and at every glimpse down the side streets and far into the distance one finds uproar, and that even so one has gone through only perhaps a quarter of populated London, you would understand that I am half out of my senses ...

...

Harriet Beecher Stowe

Harriet Beecher Stowe (1811—96), American writer, author of the great anti-slavery novel, *Uncle Tom's Cabin*, wrote this self-revelatory letter to a Mrs Follen on February 16th, 1853. The preceding month, Beecher Stowe had received a letter from Mrs Follen in London, asking for information with regard to herself, her family and the circumstances of her writing *Uncle Tom's Cabin*. When she was only seven, Beecher Stowe's father wrote in a letter, 'Harriet is a genius'. On meeting her, President Abraham Lincoln commented: 'So this is the little woman whose book brought on this big war.'

So you want to know something about what sort of a woman I am! Well, if this is any object, you shall have statistics free of charge. To begin, then, I am a little bit of a woman, — somewhat more than forty, about as thin and dry as a pinch of snuff; never very much to look at in my best days, and looking like a used-up article now.

I was married when I was twenty-five years old to a man rich in Greek and Hebrew, Latin and Arabic, and, alas! rich in nothing else. When I went to housekeeping, my entire stock of china for parlour and kitchen was bought for eleven dollars. That lasted very well for two years, till my brother was married and brought his bride to visit me. I then found, on review, that I had neither plates nor teacups to set a table for my father's family; wherefore I thought it best to reinforce the establishment by getting me a tea-set that cost ten dollars more, and this, I believe, formed my whole stock in trade for some years.

But then I was abundantly enriched with wealth of another sort. I had two little, curly-headed twin daughters to begin with, and my stock in this line has gradually increased, till I have been the mother of seven children, the most beautiful and the most loved of whom lies buried near my Cincinnati residence. It was at his dying bed and at his grave that I learned what a poor slave mother may feel when her child is torn away from her. In those depths of sorrow which seemed to me immeasurable, it was my only prayer to God that such anguish might not be suffered in vain. There were circumstances about his death of such peculiar bitterness, of what seemed almost cruel suffering, that I felt that I could never be consoled for it, unless this crushing of my own heart might enable me to work out some great good to others ...

I allude to this here because I have often felt that much that is in that book ('Uncle Tom') had its root in the awful scenes and bitter sorrows of that summer. It has left now, I trust, no trace on my mind, except a deep compassion for the sorrowful, especially for mothers who are separated from their children.

...

Charles Dickens

Charles Dickens (1812—70), English novelist, was working as a parliamentary reporter for the *Morning Chronicle* when he wrote this letter to Thomas Beard, a fellow reporter, on January 11th, 1835.

Yesterday I had to start at 8 oclock for Braintree ... and being unable to get a Saddle Horse, I actually ventured on a gig, — and what is more, I actually did the four and twenty miles without upsetting it. I wish to God you could have seen me tooling in and out of the banners, drums, conservative Emblems, horsemen, and go-carts with which every little Green was filled as the processions were waiting for Sir John Tyrell and Baring. Every time the horse heard a drum he bounded into the hedge, on the left side of the road; and every time I got him out of that, he bounded into the hedge on the right side. When he *did* go however, he went along admirably. The road was clear when I returned, and with the trifling exception of breaking my Whip, I flatter myself I did the whole thing in something like style.

If any one were to ask me what in my opinion was the dullest and most stupid spot on the face of the Earth, I should decidedly say Chelmsford. Though only 29 miles from town, there is not a single shop where they sell Sunday Papers ... And here I am on a wet Sunday looking out of a damned large bow window at the rain as it falls into the puddles opposite, wondering when it will be dinner time, and cursing my folly in having put no books into my Portmanteau ... There is not even anything to look at in the place, except two immense prisons, large enough to hold all the Inhabitants of the country ...

...

Charlotte Brontë

Charlotte Brontë (1816—55), English writer, maintained a ceaseless correspondence with her lifelong and dearest friend, Ellen Nussey. This letter dates from March 1845.

I can hardly tell you how time gets on here at Haworth — There is no event whatever to mark its progress — one day resembles another — and all have heavy, lifeless physiognomies — Sunday — baking day and Saturday are the only ones that bear the slightest distinctive mark — meantime life wears away — I shall soon be 30 — and I have done nothing yet — Sometimes I get melancholy — at the prospect before and behind me — yet it is wrong and foolish to repine — and undoubtedly my duty directs me to stay at home for the present — There was a time when Haworth was a very pleasant place to me, it is not so now — I feel as if we were all buried here — I long to travel — to work to live a life of action — Excuse me dear Ellen for troubling you with my fruitless wishes — I will put by the rest and not bother you with them.

Brontë's dissolute brother, Branwell, died on September 24th, 1848. She wrote this letter to W. S. Williams, an early admirer of *Jane Eyre*, on October 2nd, 1848.

'We have buried our dead out of sight.' A lull begins to succeed the gloomy tumult of last week. It is not permitted us to grieve for him who is gone as others grieve for those they lose. The removal of our only brother must necessarily be regarded by us rather in the light of a mercy than a chastisement. Branwell was his father's and his sisters' pride and hope in boyhood, but since manhood the case has been otherwise. It has been our lot to see him take a wrong bent; to hope, expect, wait his return to the right path; to know the sickness of hope deferred, the dismay of prayer baffled; to experience despair at last — and now to behold the sudden early obscure close of what might have been a noble career.

I do not weep from a sense of bereavement — there is no prop withdrawn, no consolation torn away, no dear companion lost — but for the wreck of talent, the ruin of promise, the untimely dreary extinction of what might have been a burning and a shining light. My brother was a year my junior. I had aspirations and ambitions for him once, long ago — they have perished mournfully. Nothing remains of him but a memory of errors and sufferings …

My unhappy brother never knew what his sisters had done in literature — he was not aware that they had ever published a line. We could not tell him of our efforts for fear of causing him too deep a pang of remorse for his own time misspent, and talents misapplied. Now he will never know. I cannot dwell longer on the subject at present — it is too painful.

...

Henry David Thoreau

Henry David Thoreau (1817—62), American writer, wrote this moving definition of happiness and loss to Lucy Brown on March 2nd, 1842. She was the sister-in-law of his friend Ralph Waldo Emerson, the great American writer. In this letter Thoreau refers to his brother, John, who had died two months previously, and to Waldo, Emerson's son, who had died two weeks after John. Thoreau was so overcome by their deaths that he did not write his journal or any letters for two months.

Soon after John's death I listened to a music-box, and if, at any time, that even had seemed inconsistent with the beauty and harmony of the universe, it was then gently constrained into the placid course of nature by those steady notes, in mild and unoffended tone echoing far and wide under the heavens. But I find these things more strange than sad to me. What right have I to grieve, who have not ceased to wonder?

We feel at first as if some opportunities of kindness and sympathy were lost, but learn afterward that any *pure grief* is ample recompense for all. That is, if we are faithful; — for a spent grief is but sympathy with the soul that disposes events, and is as natural as the resin of Arabian trees. — Only nature has a right to grieve perpetually, for she only is innocent. Soon the ice will melt, and the blackbirds sing along the river which he frequented, as pleasantly as ever. The same everlasting serenity will appear in this face of God, and we will not be sorrowful, if he is not.

We are made happy when reason can discover no occasion for it. The memory of some past moments is more persuasive than the experience of present ones. There have been visions of such breadth and brightness that these motes were invisible in their light.

I do not wish to see John ever again — I mean him who is dead — but that other whom only he would have wished to see, or to be, of whom he was the imperfect representative. For we are not what we are, nor do we treat or esteem each other for such, but for what we are capable of being.

As for Waldo, he died as the mist rises from the brook, which the sun will soon dart his rays through. Do not the flowers die every autumn? He had not even taken root here. I was not startled to hear that he was dead; — it seemed the most natural event that could happen. His fine organization demanded it, and nature gently yielded its request. It would have been strange if he had lived. Neither will nature manifest any sorrow at his death, but soon the note of the lark will be heard down in the meadow, and fresh dandelions will spring from the old stocks where he plucked them last summer. I have been living ill of late, but am now doing better. How do you live in that Plymouth world, now-a-days? — Please remember me to Mary Russell. — You must not blame me if I do *talk to the clouds*, for I remain.

Your Friend,
Henry D. Thoreau.

...

James Russell Lowell

James Russell Lowell (1819—91), American poet and critic, sent this letter to Julia Stephen (mother of Virginia Woolf and Vanessa Bell), on November 9th, 1889.

It is a very strange feeling this of renewing my life here. I feel somehow as if Charon had ferried me the wrong way, and yet it is into a world of ghosts that he has brought me, and I am slowly making myself at home among them. It is raining faintly to-day, with a soft southerly wind which will prevail with the few leaves left on my trees to let go their hold and join their fellows on the ground. I have forbidden them to be raked away, for the rustle of them stirs my earliest memories, and when the wind blows they pirouette so gaily as to give me cheerful thoughts of death. But oh, the change! I hardly know the old road (a street now) that I have paced so many years, for the new houses. My old homestead seems to have a puzzled look in its eyes as it looks down ... on these upstarts.

It is odd to think that the little feet which make the old staircases and passages querulous at their broken slumbers are the second generation since my own ... I feel so anomalously young I can't persuade myself that I ever made such a rumpus, though perhaps the boots are thicker now.

The two old English elms in front of the house haven't changed. The sturdy islanders! A trifle thicker in the waist, perhaps, as is the wont of prosperous elders, but looking just as I first saw them seventy years ago, and it is a balm to my eyes. I am by no means sure that it is wise to love the accustomed and familiar so much as I do, but it is pleasant and gives a unity to life which trying can't accomplish.

...

John Ruskin

John Ruskin (1819—1900), English writer, artist, designer and philosopher, was an inveterate writer of letters. Here is a selection of his missives, showing the diversity of his thinking and the charm of his personality.

To Edward Clayton, a college acquaintance, May 16th, 1841.

Everything disappoints one so desperately as you get up in age. That power of being happy with a few violet-seeds or foxglove-bells is so glorious in childhood — so severe a loss, no prospects of men can ever recompense it. Ambition disturbs, science fatigues, everything else cloys. Not but that I can sail a boat in a gutter or build a bridge over a rivulet still, with much delight and self-edification; but one does not like to look, even to one's reflection in the water, so like an idiot. Senses of duty and responsibility too are confounded bores. What a nice thing it was at six years old to be told everything you were to do, and whipped if you did not do it!

To Elizabeth Barrett Browning, English poet, in 1858. He had recently finished the major task of cataloguing, framing and preparing for exhibition the sketches Joseph Turner had bequeathed to the National Gallery.

I have had a cloud upon me this year, and don't quite know the meaning of it; only I've had no heart to write to anybody. I suppose the real gist of it is that next year I shall be forty, and begin to see what life and the world mean, seen from the middle of them — and the middle inclining to the dustward end. I believe there is something owing to the violent reaction after the excitement of the arrangement of Turner's sketches; something to my ascertaining in the course of that work how the old man's soul had been gradually crushed within him ... something to my having enjoyed too much of lovely things, till they almost cease to be lovely to me, and because I have no monotonous and disagreeable work by way of foil to them ...

To his father, John James Ruskin, December 1863.

I have always been so able until now to shake off regret and amuse myself with work of some sort, that now, when my mountains and cathedrals fail me, and I find myself feeling dull in a pine forest or a country town, I directly think I must be dying ... Men ought to be severely disciplined and exercised in the sternest way in daily life — they should learn to lie on stone beds and eat black soup, but they should never have their hearts broken — a noble heart, once broken, never mends ... The two terrific mistakes which Mama and you involuntarily fell into were the exact reverse in both ways — you fed me effeminately and luxuriously to the extent that I actually now could not travel in rough countries without taking a cook with me — but you thwarted me in all the earnest fire and passion of life ... if I had had courage and knowledge enough to insist on having my own way resolutely, you would now have had me in happy health, loving you twice as much ... full of energy for the future and of power and of self-denial; now, my power of *duty* has been exhausted in vain, and I am forced for life's sake to indulge myself in all sorts of selfish ways, just when a man ought to be knit for the duties of middle life by the good success of his youthful life. No life ought to have *phantoms* to lay.

...

Fyodor Mikhailovich Dostoyevsky

Fyodor Mikhailovich Dostoyevsky (1821—81), Russian novelist, wrote this letter to his brother, Mihail, on December 22nd, 1849. The novelist and a group of socialist comrades had been sentenced to death as conspirators. He was exiled to Siberia where he was imprisoned until 1854.

To-day, the 22nd of December, sentence of death was read to all of us, we were told to kiss the Cross, our swords were broken over our heads, ... Then three were tied to the pillar for execution. I was the sixth. Three at a time were called out; consequently, I was in the second batch and no more than a minute was left me to live.

I remembered you, brother, and all yours; during the last minute you, you alone, were in my mind, only then I realized how I love you, dear brother mine! ... Finally the retreat was sounded, and those tied to the pillar were led back, and it was announced to us that His Imperial Majesty granted us our lives ... I was just told, dear brother, that to-day or to-morrow we are to be sent off ... Brother! I have not become down-hearted or low-spirited. Life is everywhere life, life in ourselves, not in what is outside us. There will be people near me, and to be a *man* among people and remain a man for ever, not to be down-hearted nor to fall in whatever misfortunes may befall me — this is life; this is the task of life ...

Brother, take care of yourself and of your family, live quietly and carefully ... Live positively. There has never yet been working in me such a healthy abundance of spiritual life as now.

...

Emily Dickinson

Emily Dickinson (1830—86), American poet, was just fifteen years old when she wrote this letter to Abiah Root on January 31st, 1846. They were close friends for ten years, but the friendship appears to have lapsed after Abiah's marriage in 1854.

Does not Eternity appear dreadful to you. I often get thinking of it and it seems so dark to me that I almost wish there was no Eternity. To think that we must forever live and never cease to be. It seems as if Death which all so dread because it launches us upon an unknown world would be a relief to so endless a state of existence. I dont know why it is but it does not seem to me that I shall ever cease to live on earth — I cannot imagine with the farthest stretch of my imagination my own death scene — It does not seem to me that I shall ever close my eyes in death. I cannot realize that the grave will be my last home — that friends will weep over my coffin and that my name will be mentioned as one who has ceased to be among the haunts of the living, and it will be wondered where my disembodied spirit has flown. I cannot realize that the friends I have seen pass from my sight in the prime of their days like dew before the sun will not again walk the streets and act their parts in the great drama of life, nor can I realize that when I again meet them it will be in another & a far different world from this.

Another letter from Emily Dickinson, this time to Susan Gilbert, who married her brother, Austin Dickinson. Emily grew passionately fond of Susan and emotionally dependent upon her love. This letter is dated February 1852.

And thank you for my dear letter, which came on Saturday night, when all the world was still; thank you for the love it bore me, and for it's golden thoughts, and feelings so like gems, that I was sure I *gathered* them in whole baskets of pearls! I mourn this morning, Susie, that I have no sweet sunset to gild a page for *you*, nor any bay so blue — not even a little chamber way up in the sky, as your's is, to give me thoughts of heaven, which I would give to you. You know how I must write you, down, down, in the terrestrial; no sunset here, no stars; not even a bit of *twilight* which I may poetize — and send you! Yet Susie, there will be romance in the letter's ride to you — think of the hills and the dales, and the rivers it will pass over, and the drivers and conductors who will hurry it on to you; and wont that make a poem such as can ne'er be written?

...

Isabel Burton

Isabel Burton (1831—96) was the wife of the Victorian adventurer Richard Burton. This letter was written to her mother during a trip to Brazil in 1865.

It was fortunate that I had the foresight to take iron bedsteads along, as already at Lisbon three-inch cockroaches seethed about the floor of our room. I jumped onto a chair and Burton growled, 'I suppose you think you look very pretty standing on that chair and howling at those innocent creatures.' My reaction was to stop screaming and reflect that he was right; if I had to live in a country full of such creatures, and worse, I had better pull myself together. I got down among them, and started lashing out with a slipper. In two hours I had a bag full of 97, and had conquered my queasiness.

...

William James

William James (1842—1910), American philosopher and psychologist and brother of the writer Henry James, wrote this letter to his students at Radcliffe College on April 6th, 1896. They had presented him with an azalea plant at a university ceremony.

Dear Young Ladies,

I am deeply touched by your remembrance. It is the first time anyone ever treated me so kindly, so you may well believe that the impression on the heart of the lonely sufferer will be even more durable than the impression on your minds of all the teachings of Philosophy 2A. I now perceive one immense omission in my Psychology, — the deepest principle of Human Nature is the *craving to be appreciated*, and I left it out altogether from the book, because I had never had it gratified till now. I fear you have let loose a demon in me, and that all my actions will now be for the sake of such rewards. However, I will try to be faithful to this one unique and beautiful azalea tree, the pride of my life and delight of my existence. Winter and summer will I tend and water it — even with my tears. Mrs James shall never go near it or touch it. If it dies, I will die too; and if I die, it shall be planted on my grave.

Don't take all this too jocosely, but believe in the extreme pleasure you have caused me, and in the affectionate feelings with which I am and shall always be faithfully your friend.

...

Sarah Bernhardt

Sarah Bernhardt (1844—1923), French actress, wrote this undated letter to her beloved granddaughter, Lysiane, who was travelling in Italy with a chaperone.

I am happy to think of you in lovely sunshine and above all, in that atmosphere of beauty which pervades all Italy ... I regret not being the one to lift the mysterious veil of infinite beauty ... Take in much with your grave eyes, with your spirit and hold onto it; for it is in the light of beauty that the soul bathes and bathes again ever. Take care not to catch cold in the churches and museums. Keep your furpiece about your neck. Evenings on your friend's little balcony watch the sunsets, they must be magnificent; sketch a bit of what you see in that garden of poetry. Look at the great screen of black cypresses, look down on the little pond so ancient and charming.

...

August Strindberg

August Strindberg (1849—1912), Swedish playwright, wrote this winsome account to his unborn child on September 4th, 1901. Strindberg's wife, Harriet Bosse, gave birth to a daughter, Anne-Marie, the following spring. The marriage was a troubled one, as the journeys chronicled here indicate.

To my child! (The unborn little one)

My child! Our child! ... Our Midsummer child! Your parents walked about in their home waiting for something — and all waiting being long and frequently tedious, they imagined that they themselves were dull and tiresome.

They waited for something to arrive. They were not aware that it had come — in a quiet, fragrant room with yellow walls — yellow as gold and sun — beneath a canopy of white gauze ...

Then your Mother was gripped by a longing to see her Mother's native land — an intense longing that tore her with bleeding heart from home and hearth.

In the pale green wood of beech by the blue sea you were carried, child of North — and Southland ...

And your lovely Mother cradled you upon the blue waters that sweep three kingdoms ... and in the evenings, when the sun was about to set, then — then she sat in the garden, looking the sun in the face, that you might be given the sun to drink of.

Child of the sea and the sun, you slept your first slumber in a little red cottage of ivy, in a white room, where words of hate were not even whispered and where nothing impure was even thought ...

Then you made a dismal journey — a pilgrimage to the City of

Sin [Berlin], where your father was to weep ...

And then you came back home to the golden room, where the sun shines, through night and day, and where tenderness was waiting for you ... and then you were carried off ...

The End.

...

Calamity Jane

Calamity Jane (Martha Jane Canary) (1852—1903), American frontierswoman, became a living legend for her riding and shooting skills. She reportedly threatened 'calamity' to any man who tried to woo her, but after his murder in 1876 she claimed to have married Wild Bill Hickock in 1870. Their daughter Janey, given up for adoption, was the recipient of this letter. Calamity Jane later married Clinton Burke, a Texan.

Your picture brought back all the years I have lived with your Father and recalled how jealous I was of him. I feel like writing about him tonight so I will tell you some things you should know. I met James Butler Hickock, 'Wild Bill', in 1870 near Abeline, Kansas. I heard a bunch of outlaws planning to kill him. I couldn't get to where my horse was so I crawled on my hands and knees through the brush past the outlaws for over a mile and reached the old shack where he was staying that night. I told him and he hid me back of the door while he shot it out with them. They hit him, cutting open the top of his head and then they heard him fall and lit matches to see if he was dead. Bill killed them all. I'll never forget what he looked like with blood running down his face while he used two guns. He never aimed and I guess he was never known to have missed anyone he aimed at, I mean wanted to kill, and he only shot in self-defence. Then he was quite sure. I nursed him several days and then while on the trip to Abeline we met Rev. Sipes and Rev. Warren and we were married. There will be lots of fools doubt that but I will leave you plenty of proof that we were. You were not a woods colt Janey. Don't let any of those pusgullied [erased] ever get busy with that lie ...

...

Oscar Wilde

Oscar Wilde (1854—1900), Irish writer, was befriended by the novelist Ada Leverson. She was there to meet Wilde when he was released from prison after serving two years' hard labour for immoral practices. She was one of the few friends who remained loyal to him during his trial and disgrace. This letter is dated May 20th, 1897.

Dear Sphinx,

I was so charmed with seeing you yesterday morning that I must write a line to tell you how sweet and good it was of you to be of the very first to greet me. When I think that Sphinxes are minions of the moon, and that you got up early before dawn, I am filled with wonder and joy.

I often thought of you in the long black days and nights of my prison-life, and to find you just as wonderful and dear as ever was no surprise. The beautiful are always beautiful.

...

Sidonie-Gabrielle Colette

Sidonie-Gabrielle Colette (1873—1954), French novelist, wrote this letter to her closest friend Marguerite Moreno, French actress, on April 10th, 1923. They first met around 1894 and remained friends until Marguerite's death in 1948.

... Just imagine that I arrived home — intending to lunch alone — and I opened the drawer of my little desk to get some money — and a single letter fell out, a letter from my mother, written in pencil, one of her last, with unfinished words and an implicit sense of her departure ... It's so curious: one can resist tears and 'behave' very well in the hardest hours of grief. But then someone makes you a friendly sign behind a window — or one notices that a flower that was in bud only yesterday has suddenly blossomed, or a letter slips from a drawer — and everything collapses.

...

Vanessa Bell

Vanessa Bell (1879—1961), English painter and designer, wrote this letter about maternity to her sister, the writer Virginia Woolf, on May 3rd, 1927. They were both leading members of the Bloomsbury set of writers, artists and philosophers, a group that also included E. M. Forster, Roger Fry (Bell's lover) and Lytton Strachey.

What a lot I could say about the maternal instinct, but then also what a lot about Michael Angelo and Raphael. I wish you would write a book about the maternal instinct. In all my wide reading I haven't yet found it properly explored. You have many opportunities for observation and you can start with birth, which also has never been described except by men, or did a friend of Ray's do it the other day? Anyhow, they never know anything about it naturally, and I could tell you a great deal. Of course it is one of the worst of the passions, animal and remorseless. But how can one avoid yielding to these instincts if one happens to have them?

...

Virginia Woolf

Virginia Woolf (1882—1941), English writer, wrote this letter to her husband, Leonard, on March 28th, 1941, before her suicide. She had suffered from recurring depressions and had already attempted to take her own life in 1913. In 1941 she placed a large stone in her pocket and drowned herself in the River Ouse near her home in Sussex. Woolf's works include several volumes of letters, diaries and essays, but she is best known for her novels, such as *To the Lighthouse* and *The Waves*, and she is rightly considered one of the great innovators of the English novel.

Dearest,

I feel certain that I am going mad again. I feel we can't go through another of those terrible times. And I shan't recover this time. I begin to hear voices, and I can't concentrate. So I am doing what seems the best thing to do. You have given me the greatest possible happiness. You have been in every way all that anyone could be. I don't think two people could have been happier till this terrible disease came. I can't fight any longer. I know that I am spoiling your life, that without me you could work. And you will I know. You see I can't even write this properly. I can't read. What I want to say is I owe all the happiness of my life to you. You have been entirely patient with me and incredibly good. I want to say that — everybody knows it. If anybody could have saved me it would have been you. Everything has gone from me but the certainty of your goodness. I can't go on spoiling your life any longer.

I don't think two people could have been happier than we have been.

...

Karen Blixen

Karen Blixen (Isak Dinesen) (1885—1962), Danish novelist and storyteller, lived for a time on a coffee plantation in Kenya, but in 1931 returned to Denmark, where she wrote several books, including *Out of Africa*, which was made into a film. She wrote this letter to her mother in autumn 1921.

No doubt each of your children thinks that he or she loves you most, and so do I. It is probably not true. But each one cares for you in his or her own way, and I think that there is something in the way that I love you that resembles the way Father loved you. For me you are the most beautiful and wonderful person in the world; merely the fact that you are alive makes the whole world different; where you are there is peace and harmony, shade and flowing springs, birds singing; to come to where you are is like entering 'heaven'...

Edith Sitwell

Edith Sitwell (1887—1964), English writer and poet, was a member of a great dynasty of patrons and propagators of the arts. Sitwell's caustic sense of humour is evident in this letter to Minnie Astor, wife of the New York magnate Vincent Astor, dated April 29th, 1950. She was writing from Montegufoni in Italy.

I have been here for exactly a fortnight. But I only began to recover yesterday from my journey, which was — let us face it — sheer hell! I left a trail of despair and nervous breakdown among all the officials from Victoria to Pisa (inclusive) and my name is mud. Their descendants will probably frighten their children with my name, three generations hence, as the English used to frighten their children with the name of Napoleon.

At Victoria I lost all my permits, and it was some time before they were found. Boarding the Train Bleu, I lost my porter and my luggage — again found with difficulty. At the frontier the train was held up owing to my misdemeanours, and I was hauled out in the snow at 7.30 A.M. to have a furious row with the Custom Officials, who asked if I was opening a shop. At Pisa, where I had to alight, there was no motor. It is 2½ hours' drive over the mountains to Montegufoni, I can speak no Italian, don't know the way, there was a heavy fog, and it was nearly night. Also my luggage was (again) lost. Eventually I arrived, to find Osbert with a heavy cold and much badgered by ghosts. (A purple light got into his room at 2.30 A.M. and gave him gyp for ten minutes one night; and the next, he heard a dead person being wheeled in a trolley along the passage outside his room.)

However now all is well. The ghosts have quieted down, I have recovered my nerve, the fireflies are out, and the village band has begun to practise on lovely brass instruments under my bedroom window.

...

Katherine Mansfield

Katherine Mansfield (1888—1923), New Zealand-born writer, had a great gift for letter writing. This precociously self-aware letter was sent to her schoolfriend, Sylvia Payne, who was also her second cousin, on December 23rd, 1903.

I like you much more than any other girl I have met in England & I seem to see less of you. We just stand upon the threshold of each other's heart and never get right in. What I mean by 'heart' is just this. My heart is a place where everything I love (whether it be in imagination or in truth) has a free entrance. It is where I store my memories, all my happiness and my sorrow and there is a large compartment in it labelled *'Dreams'*. There are many many people that I like very much, but they generally view my public rooms, and they call me false, and mad, and changeable. I would not show them what I was really like for worlds. They would think me madder I suppose —

I wish we could know each other, so that I might be able to say 'Sylvia is one of my *best* friends.' Don't think that I mean half I look and say to other people. I cannot think why I so seldom am myself. I think I rather hug myself to myself, too much. Don't you? Not that it is beautiful or precious. It is a very shapeless, bare, undecorated thing just yet.

Fifteen years later, when in the grip of her illness, Mansfield wrote this letter to Lady Ottoline Morrell, society hostess to the Bloomsbury set.

I know so devilishly well the agony of feeling perpetually ill and the longing — the immense longing — just to have what everybody else takes so easily as their portion — health — a body that isn't an enemy — a body that isn't fiendishly engaged in the old, old 'necessary' torture of — breaking ones spirit — 'Why wont you consent to having your spirit broken?' it wonderingly asks. 'Everybody else yields without a murmur. And if you'd only realize the comfortable, boundless numbness that you would enjoy for ever after —' I wonder sometimes how it will end. One will never give in and so — All the same, it would be more tolerable if only people understood— ever so little — but *subtly* — not with a sort of bread jelly sympathy — but with exquisite, rare friendship.

...

Vita Sackville-West

Vita Sackville-West (1892—1962), aristocratic English writer and gardener, enjoyed an open but affectionate marriage with Harold Nicolson. He had just returned to Berlin where he was at the start of a brilliant diplomatic career. Sackville-West, however, did not go with him as she found the diplomatic life and its formalities unbearable. Both were unhappy and this emotional letter to him, dated June 25th, 1929, was possibly not without importance in his decision to resign from his post.

What is so torturing when I leave you at these London stations and drive off, is the knowledge that you are *still* there — that, for half an hour or three-quarters of an hour, I could still return and find you: come up behind you, take you by the elbow, and say 'Hadji'.

I came straight home, feeling horribly desolate and sad, driving down that familiar and dreary road. I remembered Rasht and our parting there: our parting at Victoria when you left for Persia; till our life seemed made up of partings, and I wondered how long it would continue ...

Then I came home, and it was no consolation at all. You see, when I am unhappy for other reasons, the cottage is a real solace to me; but when it is on account of you that I am unhappy (because you have gone away), it is an additional pang — it is the same place, but a sort of mockery and emptiness hangs about it — I almost wish that just *once* you could lose me and then come straight back to the cottage and find it still full of me but empty of me, then you would know what I go through after you have gone away.

...

Nadezhda Mandelstam

Nadezhda Mandelstam (1899—1980) wrote this letter to her husband, the poet Osip Mandelstam, in October 1938. They met in May 1919. Nineteen years later she saw Stalin's secret police take him away in a truck. He never came back. This letter probably expresses the feelings of many women who shared her fate, losing their lovers, husbands, brothers or sons, but it is unusual because it has survived. A few months after writing it she learned that her husband was dead and the letter was put away for decades. Only after many years did Nadezhda Mandelstam find the strength and courage to reread it and publish it in her book *Hope Abandoned*.

Osia, my beloved, faraway sweetheart!

I have no words, my darling, to write this letter that you may never read, perhaps. I am writing it into empty space. Perhaps you will come back and not find me here. Then this will be all you have left to remember me by.

Osia, what a joy it was living together like children — all our squabbles and arguments, the games we played, and our love. Now I do not even look at the sky. If I see a cloud, who can I show it to?

Each letter you send me penetrates more deeply into my heart

Gustave Flaubert, French writer, author of *Madame Bovary*,
to Louise Colet, French poet, August 12th, 1846.

Human Creativity

Sir, more than kisses,
letters mingle souls

John Donne (1572 —1631)
English poet and cleric

Jonathan Swift

Jonathan Swift (1667—1745), Irish writer, sent this letter to Benjamin Motte, bookseller and publisher of *Gulliver's Travels*, on August 8th, 1726. So afraid was Swift of government prosecution for the stinging political satire in his book, that he adopted the pseudonym of Richard Sympson even when writing to his publisher. He also published the book under the name of its hero, Lemuel Gulliver. Nor was the letter written in his own hand — Swift dictated it to his friend, the writer John Gay.

My Cousin Mr Lemuel Gulliver entrusted me some Years ago with a Copy of his Travels, whereof that which I here send you is about a fourth part, for I shortned them very much as you will find in my Preface to the Reader. I have shewn them to several persons of great Judgment and Distinction, who are confident they will sell very well. And although some parts of this and the following Volumes may be thought in one or two places to be a little Satyrical, yet it is agreed they will give no Offence, but in that you must Judge for your self ... The good Report I have received of you makes me put so great a trust into your Hands, which I hope you will give me no Reason to repent, and in that Confidence I require that you will never suffer these Papers to be once out of your Sight.

As the printing these Travels will probably be of great value to you, so as a Manager for my Friend and Cousin I expect you will give a due consideration for it, because I know the Author intends the profit for the use of poor Sea-men, and I am advised to say that two Hundred pounds is the least Summ I will receive on his account ...

If you do not approve of this proposal deliver these Papers to the person who will come on thursday.

If you chuse rather to send the Papers make no other Proposal of your own but just barely write on a piece of paper that you do not accept my offer.

...

George Frederick Handel

George Frederick Handel (1685—1759), German composer, sent this letter to his patron, Charles Jennens, on September 13th, 1744. Jennens helped with the *libretti* for some of Handel's oratorios, including the one referred to in this letter, *Belshazzar*.

Your most excellent Oratorio has given me great Delight in setting it to Musick and still engages me warmly. It is indeed a Noble Piece, very grand and uncommon, it has furnished me with Expressions, and has given me Opportunity to some very particular Ideas, besides so many great Choruses. I entreat you heartily to favour me soon with the last Act, which I expect with anxiety, that I may regulate my Self the better as to the Length of it. I profess my Self highly obliged to you, for so generous a Present ...

...

Voltaire (François-Marie Arouet)

Voltaire (François-Marie Arouet) (1694—1778), French writer and philosopher, protested to a government official about the severe censorship in the press in the eighteenth century. Many nonconformist writers of the time had their works destroyed and were often forced to flee Paris for fear of punishment. This letter is dated June 20th, 1733.

As you have it in your power, sir, to do some service to letters, I implore you not to clip the wings of our writers so closely, nor to turn into barn-door fowls those who, allowed a start, might become eagles; reasonable liberty permits the mind to soar — slavery makes it creep.

Had there been a literary censorship in Rome, we should have had to-day neither Horace, Juvenal, nor the philosophical works of Cicero ...

A great library is like the City of Paris, in which there are about eight hundred thousand persons: you do not live with the whole crowd: you choose a certain society, and change it. So with books: you choose a few friends out of the many. There will be seven or eight thousand controversial books, and fifteen or sixteen thousand novels, which you will not read ... The man of taste will only read what is good; but the statesman will permit both bad and good.

Men's thoughts have become an important article of commerce. The Dutch publishers make a million [francs] a year, because Frenchmen have brains. A feeble novel is, I know, among books what a fool, always striving after wit, is in the world. We laugh at him and tolerate him. Such a novel brings the means of life to the author who wrote it, the publisher who sells it, to the moulder, the printer, the paper-maker, the binder, the carrier — and finally to the bad wine-shop where they all take their money ... Thus, despicable though it may be, it will have produced two important things — profit and pleasure.

...

Samuel Johnson

Samuel Johnson (1709—84), English writer and critic, originally petitioned the Earl of Chesterfield to be the patron of his work in progress, the *English Dictionary*. He was ignored until the work was published and Chesterfield sought association. The

Earl wrote two rather condescending essays, prompting the following letter from Johnson, who now considered himself 'an oracle of literature' and no longer needy of illustrious patrons.

My Lord,

I have been lately informed, by the proprietor of the *World*, that two papers, in which my Dictionary is recommended to the publick, were written by your Lordship. To be so distinguished, is an honour, which, being very little accustomed to favours from the great, I know not well how to receive, or in what terms to acknowledge.

When, upon some slight encouragement, I first visited your Lordship, I was overpowered, like the rest of mankind, by the enchantment of your address; and could not forebear to wish that I might boast myself *Le vainqueur du vainqueur de la terre*; — that I might obtain that regard for which I saw the world contending; but I found my attendance so little encouraged, that neither pride nor modesty would suffer me to continue it. When I had once addressed your Lordship in publick, I had exhausted all the art of pleasing which a retired and uncourtly scholar can possess. I had done all that I could; and no man is well pleased to have his all neglected, be it ever so little.

Seven years, my Lord, have now past, since I waited in your outward rooms, or was repulsed from your door; during which time I have been pushing on my work through difficulties, of which it is useless to complain, and have brought it, at last, to the verge of publication, without one act of assistance, one word of encouragement, or one smile of favour. Such treatment I did not expect, for I never had a Patron before ...

Is not a Patron, my Lord, one who looks with unconcern on a man struggling for life in the water, and, when he has reached ground, encumbers him with help? The notice which you have been pleased to take of my labours, had it been early, had been kind; but it has been delayed till I am indifferent, and cannot enjoy it; till I am solitary, and cannot impart it; till I am known, and do not want it. I hope it is no very cynical asperity not to confess obligations where no benefit has been received, or to be unwilling that the Publick should consider me as owing that to a Patron, which Providence has enabled me to do for myself.

Having carried on my work thus far with so little obligation to any favourer of learning, I shall not be disappointed though I should conclude it, if less be possible, with less; for I have been long wakened from that dream of hope, in which I once boasted myself with so much exhultation.

...

Catherine Clive

Catherine Clive (1711—85), English actress, wrote this letter to David Garrick, English actor, manager and dramatist, on June 23ʳᵈ, 1776, when she heard that Garrick had decided to retire from the stage and management after an immensely successful career. Kitty Clive performed regularly at Drury Lane for 40 years. 'Pivy' was Garrick's pet name for the actress.

Is it really true that you have put an end to the glory of Drury Lane Theatre? *If it is so*, let me congratulate my dear Mr and Mrs Garrick on their approaching happiness. I *know* what it will be: you cannot yet have an idea of it; but if you should still be so wicked not to be satisfied with that *unbounded*, uncommon degree of fame you have received as an actor, and which no other actor ever did receive — nor no other actor ever *can* receive — I say, if you should still long to be dipping your fingers in their theatrical pudding (now without plums), you will be no Garrick for the Pivy.

In the height of public admiration for you — when you were never mentioned with any other appellation but Mr Garrick the charming man, the fine fellow, the delightful creature, both by men and ladies, when they were admiring everything you did and everything you scribbled — at this very time *the Pivy* was a living witness that they did not know, nor could they be sensible of, half your perfections.

I have seen you with your magical hammer in your hand, endeavouring to beat your ideas into the heads of creatures who had none of their own. I have seen you with lamb-like patience endeavouring to make them comprehend you, and I have seen you when that could not be done. I have seen your lamb turned into a lion.

...

Christoph Willibald Gluck

Christoph Willibald Gluck (1714—87), German composer, wrote this severe letter to Duke Don Giovanni di Braganza on October 30ᵗʰ, 1770. Gluck left his native Bavaria and travelled extensively in Europe, writing operas and teaching music. His most illustrious pupil was Marie-Antoinette, who married Louis XVI of France.

The more one seeks truth and perfection, the more necessary it is to be precise and exact. The qualities which distinguish Raphael from a dozen other painters are imperceptible, and, any alteration of contour, which might be permissible in caricature, would wholly disfigure the portrait of a beautiful woman. Little or nothing, apart from a slight alteration in the mode of expression, would be needed to turn my aria in *Orfeo, Che faro senze Euridice?* into a puppet dance ... And when it is a question of executing music written according to the principles I have laid down, the presence of the composer is, so to speak, as necessary as the presence of the sun to the works of nature. He is the absolute life and soul, and without him everything remains in confusion and darkness. But one must be prepared for these obstacles as long as one lives in the same world with people who feel they have the authority to judge the fine arts just because they are privileged to possess a pair of eyes and a pair of ears, no matter which.

The composer later wrote to Countess von Fries on November 16th, 1777, referring to his opera, *Armide*. Nicola Piccinni was his great rival.

The Neapolitan Ambassador, to ensure great success for Piccinni's opera, is tirelessly intriguing against me, at Court and among the nobility. He has induced Marmontel, La Harpe and several members of the Academy to write against my system of music and my manner of composing. The Abbé Arnaud, M. Suard and several others have come to my defence, and the quarrel grew so heated that from insults they would have passed to blows, but that friends of both sides brought them to order. The *Journal de Paris* which comes out every day, is full of it. This dispute is making the Editor's fortune, for he already has more than 2,500 subscribers in Paris ... Enthusiasts tell me: Sir, you are fortunate to be enjoying the honour of persecution; every great genius has had the same experience. — I wish them to the devil with their fine speeches. The fact is that the opera, which was said to have fallen flat, brought in 37,200 *livres* in 7 performances, without counting the boxes rented for the year, and without the subscribers. Yesterday at the 8th performance, they took 5,767 *livres* ... The pit was so tightly packed that when a man who had his hat on his head was told by the guard to take it off, he replied: 'Come and take it off yourself, for I cannot move my arms'; which caused laughter. I have seen people coming out with their hair bedraggled and their clothes drenched as though they had fallen into a stream. Only Frenchmen would pay so dearly for a pleasure. There are passages in the opera which force the audience to lose their countenance and their composure. Come yourself, Madame, to witness the tumult; it will amuse you as much as the opera ...

...

Thomas Gainsborough

Thomas Gainsborough (1727—88), English painter, wrote this letter to William Jackson, composer and amateur painter, on June 4th, some time before 1778.

I'm sick of Portraits and wish very much to take my Viol da Gamba and walk off to some sweet Village where I can paint Landskips and enjoy the fag End of Life in quietness and ease. But these fine Ladies and their Tea drinkings, Dancings, *Husband huntings* and such will fob me out of the last ten years, & I fear miss getting Husbands too — But we can say nothing to these things you know Jackson, we must jogg on and be content with the jingling of the Bells, only d-mn it I hate a dust, the Kicking up of a dust, and being confined *in Harness* to follow the track, whilst others ride in the waggons, under cover, stretching their Legs in the straw at Ease, and gazing at Green Trees & Blue skies without half my *Taste*, that's damn'd hard. My Comfort is, I have 5 Viols da Gamba ...

...

Franz Josef Haydn

Franz Josef Haydn (1732—1809), Austrian composer, described his admiration for Mozart to a provincial administrator, Herr Roth, in December 1787. Haydn had met Mozart on a visit to Vienna. The respect and admiration between the two composers was mutual.

... If I could but impress the matchless works of Mozart upon the souls of all music-lovers, and particularly of the Great, so deeply and with such understanding and sensibility as that with which I myself appreciate, and comprehend them, the Nations would vie with one another to possess such a treasure within their walls. Prague must hold the dear fellow — but reward him too, for without that, the history of great geniuses is melancholy and gives posterity little encouragement to further effort; on which account, alas, so many promising minds fall short of fulfilment.

...

Hester Thrale

Hester Thrale (1741—1821), English woman of letters, described the celebrated actress Mrs Siddons to her friend, Mrs Pennington, in July 1801. Hester Thrale was first married to a *bon vivant* brewer and then to an Italian violinist. For this breach of etiquette she was shunned by society, including her former great admirer Samuel Johnson.

Poor dear pretty Siddons! What has she been doing to her mouth? Picking it, my master says, as I do my fingers, which, he threatens me, are one day to resemble poor Mr. Pennington's toes. But in earnest and true sadness, what can be the matter with her lips? Lips that never were equalled in enunciation of tenderness or sublimity! Lips that spoke so kindly *to* me and *of* me! Dear soul! what can ail her? She dreamed once that all her teeth came out upon the stage I remember; I told her she would go on acting till age had bereft her of them.

Mrs Thrale was even more demonstrative in this letter to the English novelist and diarist Fanny Burney, written some time in 1782. Here she praises Fanny Burney's novel, *Cecilia*, published that year.

My eyes red with reading and crying, I stop every moment to kiss the book and to wish it was my Burney! 'Tis the sweetest book, the most interesting, the most engaging. Oh! it beats every other book, even your own other vols., for 'Evelina' was a baby to it.

Dear charming creature! do I stop every six pages to exclaim ... Such a novel! Indeed, I am seriously and sensibly touched by it, and am proud of her friendship who so knows the human heart. May mine long bear the inspection of so penetrating, so discriminating an eye!

This letter is written by scraps and patches, but every scrap is admiration, and every patch thanks you for the pleasure I have received. I will say no more; I cannot say half I think with regard to praise.

...

John Keats

John Keats (1795—1821), English poet, recorded his theories of intellectual pursuits in letters to his publisher, John Taylor. Here are some examples.

February 27th, 1818.

Poetry should strike the reader as a wording of his own highest thoughts, and appear almost a remembrance.

April 24th, 1818.

I was purposing to travel over the north this summer — there is but one thing to prevent me — I know nothing I have read nothing and I mean to follow Solomon's directions of 'get Wisdom — get understanding' — I find cavalier days are gone by. I find that I can have no enjoyment in the World but continual drinking of Knowledge — I find there is no worthy pursuit but the idea of doing some good for the world — some do it with their society — some with their wit — some with their benevolence ... there is but one way for me — the road lies through application study and thought. I will pursue it and to that end purpose retiring for some years. I have been hovering for some time between an exquisite sense of the luxurious and a love for Philosophy — were I calculated for the former I should be glad — but as I am not I shall turn all my soul to the latter.

...

Mary Shelley

Mary Shelley (1797—1851) was a prolific writer of fiction, travel books, dramas, essays, reviews and poems. She was also an inexhaustible writer of letters to her many friends. This letter was sent to her friend, Maria Gisborne, on June 11th, 1835.

You speak of women's intellect — We can scarcely do more than judge by ourselves — I know that however clever I may be there is in me a vacillation, a weakness, a want of 'eagle winged' resolution that appertains to my intellect as well as my moral character — & renders me what I am — one of broken purposes — failing thoughts & a heart all wounds. — My Mother had more energy of character — still she had not sufficient fire of imagination — In short my belief is — whether there be sex in souls or not — that the sex of our material mechanism makes us quite different creatures — better though weaker but wanting in the higher grades of intellect.

...

Harriet Martineau

Harriet Martineau (1802—76), English writer on politics and economics and advocate for women's rights, initiated a correspondence with the English poet Elizabeth Barrett in 1843, when they were both invalids. They lost contact after Barrett married Robert Browning in 1846. Here are two extracts from Martineau's letters.

August 1st, 1843.

Such a liberty as I am taking would be quite inexcusable if I could feel that we were perfect strangers. My intention is to ask your kind acceptance of a little volume of mine, written several years ago, but still in favour with the public. It is so probable that it may not suit your views or tastes that I hope & entreat that you will not think it necessary to say a word to me about it, or even to acknowledge its arrival. It if should fail to interest you entirely, I shall still not repent sending you some token of my respect and admiration, — & I may add, — sympathy. — I owe to you many many moments of pleasure, some ideas (rare gifts in this age!) & no small feeling of complacency from your permission to my dear Mrs Reid to bring me your very noble poem, Pan Departed. The stanzas of that poem have run in my head, & raised my thought, ever since the first reading; & with every revival of the impression, my gratitude to you revives.

April 18th, 1845.

Wordsworth was an educator of infinite value to me, — a worthy idol during many of the best years of my life. I do not think more highly — of his works & mind as I grow older & learn more of the modes of thought & emotion of other national & indivl minds: & in his poetry I find my pleasures arise more from the echoes of old raptures than from new disclosures.

Harriet Martineau did not hesitate to patronize the English cookery writer Isabella Beeton (1836—65), as this letter dated March 4th, 1862 shows quite clearly. One suspects that Mrs Beeton was quite sincere in her polite request to Martineau not to write.

I have never had any idea of taking advantage of your kind thoughtfulness in desiring me not to write, even to acknowledge your book: but I have waited to read it, or as much of it as is meant to be *read*, properly speaking. In my feeble condition, I feel it allowable, in a general way, to acknowledge the arrival of this sort of gift by the hand of my niece before reading them: but your book tempted me to wait, and finally write myself. It has given me a great deal of pleasure, and my niece, who relieves me of housekeeping, and is a first rate housewife, declares the book to be very valuable indeed in the cookery part. To us it seems new to state the cost of the dishes, and to the last degree useful. In course of time we shall have gone over a great deal of your ground with much thankfulness to you.

The specifications of the duties of Servants are excellent too. The parts we least like are the instructions on Manners, and in Medical matters. Being homeopaths, we think the latter very dangerous — while aware that that part is from a professional hand. I just say this much for honesty's sake, and because I know, from my own experience, that one is glad to hear what people think, when a second edition of one's book may afford an opportunity for reconsideration — whether one remains finally of the same opinion or not.

In nineteen twentieths of the book I think we may delight and rejoice; and I heartily wish you joy of it.

...

George Sand

George Sand (Amantine Aurore Dudevant) (1804—76) maintained a correspondence with fellow French writer Gustave Flaubert. This letter is dated September 21st, 1866.

It is my opinion that it is only natural that men of intelligence should display inquisitiveness. I never myself displayed any, perhaps from want of courage. I have preferred to leave my mind incomplete; that was my own affair, for we are all free to embark on a large full-rigged ship or on a little fishing-smack; just as we please. The *artiste* is an explorer who should allow nothing to daunt him, and who does neither good nor harm by searching in all directions; his object sanctifies all he does. It is his business to ascertain, after a little experience, what is the real state of health of his soul.

...

Felix Mendelssohn-Bartholdy

Felix Mendelssohn-Bartholdy (1809—47), German composer, described his experiences in England in this letter to his mother, dated June 21st, 1842.

I had to play to an audience of 3,000 people in Exeter Hall, and they cheered me with 'Hurrahs' and waved their handkerchiefs and stamped their feet until the whole place rang with it — I noticed no ill effect at the time, but next morning my head felt dizzy, as though I had not slept. And then there is the sweet, pretty Queen Victoria, who is so girlish and shyly friendly and polite, and speaks German so well, and knows all my things so well ... Only yesterday evening I was at the Palace, where the Queen and Prince Albert were almost by themselves, and she sat down beside the piano while I played to her ...

...

Margaret Fuller

Margaret Fuller (1810—50), American writer and critic, disappointed her father by being born a girl, but he still ensured that she received a rigorous education. By the time she was fifteen, she was already reading literature and philosophy in four languages. She was the first woman admitted to Harvard University, and her position as foreign correspondent on the *New York Tribune* took her to Rome, where she met the Marquis Giovanni Angelo Ossoli, who was to become her husband. She drowned in a shipwreck in 1850. Here are some samples of her letters to friends.

To Caroline Sturgis, January 27th, 1839.

I love the love lit dome above. I cannot live without mine own particular star; but my foot is on the earth and I wish to walk over it until my wings be grown. I will use my microscope as well as my telescope, and oh ye flowers, ye fruits, and, nearer kindred yet, stones with your veins so worn by fire and water, and here and there disclosing streaks of golden ore, let us know one another before we part. Tell me your secret, tell me mine. To be human is also something?

To Elizabeth Hoar, May 15th, 1839.

I have thought of many things I might have told you, but I could not bear to be eloquent and poetical. It seems all mockery thus to play the artist with life, and dip the brush in one's own heart's blood. One would fain be no more an artist, or a philosopher, or a lover, or a critic, but a soul ever rushing forth in tides of genial life, or retiring evermore into precious crystals, too pure to be lonely.

...

Elizabeth Gaskell

Elizabeth Gaskell (1810—65), English writer, had strong views on literature, as these letters show.

To Eliza Fox, December 24th or 25th, 1854.

I've been sick of writing, and everything connected with literature or improvement of the mind; to say nothing of deep hatred to my species about whom I was obliged to write as if I loved 'em. Moreover I have had to write so hard that I have spoilt my hand, and forgotten all my spelling. Seriously it has been a terrible weight on me and has made me have some of the most felling headaches I ever had in my life, so having growled my growl I'll go on to something else.

To her sister-in-law, Anne Robson, May 1865. Mrs Gaskell wrote an acclaimed biography of Charlotte Brontë two years after the novelist's death.

I HATE photographs & moreover disapprove of biographies of *living* people. I always let people *invent* mine, & have often learnt some curious particulars about myself from what they choose to say.

...

John Ruskin

John Ruskin (1819—1900), English writer, artist, designer and philosopher wrote this letter to Edward Burne-Jones, English painter, in 1877. The American painter James Whistler had threatened to bring an action for libel after Ruskin had written of his *Nocturne in Black and Gold*, 'I never expected a coxcomb to ask two hundred guineas for flinging a pot of paint in the public's face.' Whistler eventually obtained a farthing damages and each side had to pay their own costs.

It's mere nuts and nectar to me, the notion of having to answer for myself in court, and the whole thing will enable me to assert some principles of art economy which I've never got into the public's head, by writing, but may get sent over all the world vividly in a newspaper report or two.

Clara Wieck Schumann

Clara Wieck Schumann (1819—96), German child prodigy, famous concert pianist and wife of the composer Robert Schumann, described the rigours of a musical career to her youngest son, Felix, in this letter dated May 11th, 1867. After the death of her husband in 1856 she continued her career as a concert pianist in order to support her family of seven children. Although her work often separated her from the children, she was anxious to maintain contact and guide them. Felix was twelve years old when this letter was written. He became not a musician but a lawyer.

... I am writing to-day chiefly because of something which touches me very nearly. Grandmother and Ferdinand tell me that you are thinking of becoming a violinist. This would be a very serious step, more so than you may imagine. However good your work might be, if it were not quite outstanding, the part which the son of Robert Schumann would play in the world would be invidious. I would impress upon you that with your name you are justified in choosing a musical career only if you are a genius, and in addition work enormously hard. Although I am quite convinced that your talent is sufficient to afford you and others pleasure if you use it as an amateur (but even for this you must do hard work), I am equally sure that your gifts are not such as will carry you to the summits of art. I therefore beg you to think it well over, my beloved Felix. You have so many other gifts that you might choose almost any other career, and perhaps distinguish yourself in it (whatever it may be) — of course, always provided that you work very hard.

...

Count Leo Tolstoy

Count Leo Tolstoy (1828—1910), Russian novelist, wrote this self-effacing letter to W. R. S. Ralston, scholar of Russian, on October 27th, 1878. Ralston was writing an article on Tolstoy and had asked him for some biographical information. After Tolstoy's refusal, Ralston finally managed to obtain the details from Ivan Turgenev.

I am very sorry not to be able to give you a satisfactory answer to your letter. The reason of it is that I very much doubt my being an author of such importance as to interest by the incidents of my life not only the Russian, but also the European public. I am fully convinced by many examples of writers, of whom their contemporaries made very much of and which were quite forgotten in their lifetime, that for contemporaries it is impossible to judge rightly on the merits of literary works, and therefore, notwithstanding my wishes, I cannot partake the temporary illusion of some friends of mine, which seem to be sure that my works must occupy some place in the Russian literature. Quite sincerely not knowing if my works shall be read after a hundred years, or will be forgotten in a hundred days, I do not wish to take a ridiculous part in the very probable mistake of my friends.

...

Louisa May Alcott

Louisa May Alcott (1832—88), American writer, author of *Little Women*, sent this letter to Miss Churchill, a young woman seeking her advice, on December 25th, 1878.

I can only say to you as I do the many young writers who ask for advice — There is no easy road to successful authorship; it has to be earned by long & patient labor, many disappointments, uncertainties & trials. Success is often a lucky accident, coming to those who may not deserve it, while others who do have to wait & hope till they have *earned* it. That is the best sort & the most enduring.

I worked for twenty years poorly paid, little known, & quite without any ambition but to eke out a living, as I chose to support myself & began to do it at sixteen. This long drill was of use, & when I wrote *Hospital Sketches* by the beds of my soldier boys in the shape of letters home I had no idea that I was taking the first step toward what is called fame. It nearly cost my life but I discovered the secret of winning the ear & touching the heart of the public by simply telling the comic & pathetic incidents of life.

Little Women was written when I was ill, & to prove that I could *not* write books for girls. The publisher thought it *flat*, so did I, & neither hoped much for or from it. We found out our mistake, & since then, though I do not enjoy writing 'moral tales' for the young, I do it because it pays well.

But the success I value most was making my dear mother happy in her last years & taking care of my family. The rest soon grows wearisome & seems very poor beside the comfort of being an earthly Providence to those we love.

I hope you will win this joy at least, & think you *will*, for you seem to have got on well so far, & the stories are better than many sent me. I like the short one best. Lively tales of home-life or children go well, & the *Youth's Companion* is a good paying paper. I do not like Loring as he is neither honest nor polite. I have had dealings with him & know. Try Roberts Brothers 299 Washington St. They are very kind & just & if the book suits will give it a fair chance. With best wishes for a prosperous & happy New Year I am your friend.

L. M. A.

...

Piotr Ilyich Tchaikovsky

Piotr Ilyich Tchaikovsky (1840—93), Russian composer, found a benefactress in Nadejda von Meck. It seems that she fell in love with him and his music, and supported, consoled and mothered him, wrote him almost daily letters, arranged his daily life, but never talked with him face to face. Their correspondence began in 1876, when Tchaikovsky was 36 and Nadejda von Meck, 45. The homosexual Tchaikovsky had reluctantly married Antonina Ivanovna Miliukova in July 1877. After two terrifying weeks with his bride, he tried unsuccessfully to drown himself. Von Meck suddenly terminated their relationship and her financial support after twelve years, possibly because she had finally heard of his sexual orientation. The break caused endless misery to the composer. This letter is dated October 10th, 1879.

I am tremendously elated that you are satisfied with the arrangement, which in truth is well and skilfully done.

As for the music itself, I knew beforehand that you would like it; how could it have been otherwise? I wrote it with you constantly in mind. At that time, I was not nearly so intimate with you as now, but already I sensed vaguely that no one in the world could respond more keenly to the deepest and most secret gropings of my soul. No musical dedication has ever been more seriously meant. It was spoken not only on my part but on yours; the symphony was not, in truth, mine but ours. For ever it will remain my favourite work, as the monument of a time when upon a deep, insidiously growing mental disease, upon a whole series of unbearable sufferings, grief and despair, suddenly, hope dawned and the sun of happiness began to shine — and that sun was embodied in the person to whom the symphony was dedicated.

...

Leos Janácek

Leos Janácek (1854—1928), Czech composer, was 63 when he fell in love with a married woman, Kamila Stösslová. He adopted her as his muse. This letter is dated June 1928.

Today at my place (the Moravian Quartet) played our quartet *Intimate Letters*. They play it with ardour, as if they themselves were writing such 'intimate letters' ... I listened to their playing today. I listen. Did I write that? Those cries of joy, but what a strange thing, also cries of terror after a lullaby. Exultation, a warm declaration of love, imploring; untamed longing. Resolution, relentlessly to fight with the world over you. Moaning, confiding, fearing. Crushing everything beneath me if it resisted. Standing in wonder before you at our first meeting. Amazement at your appearance; as if it had fallen to the bottom of a well and from that very moment I drank the water of that well. Confusion and high-pitched song of victory ...

...

Oscar Wilde

Oscar Wilde (1854—1900), Irish novelist and playwright, described the curious public morality in England in this letter to his friend, the artist Will Rothenstein. It was written some time in 1892.

The curious thing is this: all the arts are free in England, except the actor's art; it is held by the Censor that the stage degrades and that the actors desecrate fine subjects — so the Censor prohibits not the publication of *Salome* but its production: yet, not one single actor has protested against this insult to the stage — not even Irving, who is always prating about the art of the actor — this shows how few actors are artists. All the *dramatic* critics except Archer of *The World* agree with the Censor that there should be a censorship over actors and acting! This shows how bad our stage must be, and also shows how Philistine the English journalists are.

The following letter was written by Wilde on June 9th, 1897, soon after he had been released from prison where he had served two years' hard labour for immoral practices.

I know, dear Will, you will be pleased to know that I have not come out of prison an embittered or disappointed man. On the contrary. In many ways I have gained much. I am not really ashamed of having been in prison: I often was in more shameful places: but I *am* really ashamed of having led a life unworthy of an artist. I don't say that Messalina is a better companion that Sporus, or that the one is all right and the other all wrong: I know simply that a life of definite and studied materialism, and philosophy of appetite and cynicism, and a cult of sensual and senseless ease, are bad things for an artist: they narrow the imagination and dull the more delicate sensibilities. I was all wrong, my dear boy, in my life. I was not getting the best out of me. *Now*, I think that with good health, and the friendship of a few good, simple, nice fellows like yourself, and a quiet mode of living, with isolation for thought, and freedom from the endless hunger for pleasures that wreck the body and imprison the soul, well, I think I may do things yet, that you all may like.

...

Joseph Conrad

Joseph Conrad (Josef Teodor Konrad Korzeniowski) (1857—1924), Polish-born British novelist, wrote to the English writer John Galsworthy around July 20th, 1900 to describe how he finished 'L. J.', his novel *Lord Jim*, which was published that year.

The end of *L. J.* has been pulled off with a steady drag of 21 hours. I sent wife and child out of the house (to London) and sat down at 9 A. M. with a desperate resolve to be done with it. Now and then I took a walk round the house, out at one door in at the other. Ten-minute meals. A great hush. Cigarette ends growing into a mound similar to a cairn over a dead hero. Moon rose over the barn, looked in at the window and climbed out of sight. Dawn broke, brightened. I put the lamp out and went on, with the morning breeze blowing the sheets of the MS. all over the room. Sun rose. I wrote the last word and went into the dining-room. Six o'clock I shared a piece of cold chicken with Escamillo (who was very miserable and in want of sympathy, having missed the child dreadfully all day). Felt very well, only sleepy: had a bath at seven and at 1.30 was on my way to London.

...

Eleonora Duse

Eleonora Duse (1859—1924), Italian actress, described the art of acting to the Marchese d'Arcais in 1884. 'La Duse' rose to fame in Italy and then triumphed all over Europe and in America. She was the lover and muse of the poet Gabriele D'Annunzio.

Acting — what an ugly word! If it were merely a question of 'acting', I feel that I could never have done it, and could never do it again. But the poor woman in the plays I have acted so got into my heart and mind that I had to think out the best way of making them understood by my audience, as if I were trying to comfort them ... But in the end it is generally they who comfort me. How and why and when this inexplicable reciprocity of feeling between these women and myself began; that story would be far too wearisome — and difficult as well — if I were to tell it fully.

...

Marie Bashkirtseff

Marie Bashkirtseff (1860—84), Russian artist and diarist, wrote a famous fan letter to Guy de Maupassant, French writer, around 1883/4. Her letters and diaries provide a valuable insight into the literary and artistic world of Europe in the late nineteenth century.

I read your works, I might almost say, with delight. In truth to nature, which you copy with religious fidelity, you find an inspiration that is truly sublime, while you move your readers by touches of feeling so profoundly human, that we fancy we see ourselves depicted in your pages, and love you with an egotistical love. Is this an unmeaning compliment? Be indulgent, it is sincere in the main.

You will understand that I should like to say many fine and striking things to you, but it is rather difficult, all at once, in this way. I regret this all the more as you are sufficiently great to inspire one with romantic dreams of becoming the confidante of your beautiful soul, always supposing your soul to be beautiful.

...

William Butler Yeats

William Butler Yeats (1865—1939), Irish poet, dramatist, theatre director and critic, wrote this letter to the English actress Mrs Patrick Campbell around 1901. Yeats was awarded the Nobel prize for literature in 1923.

You will permit me, however, to thank you by letter for the performance of today. Your acting seemed to me to have the perfect precision and delicacy of every art at its best. It made me feel the unity of the Arts in a new way. I said to myself 'That is exactly what I am trying to do in writing. To express oneself without waste, without emphasis. To be impassioned and yet to have a perfect self-possession. To have a precision so absolute that the slightest inflection of the voice, the slightest rhythm of sound or of motion plucks the heart strings!'

...

Virginia Woolf

Virginia Woolf (1882—1941) wrote a memorable series of letters to fellow English writer Vita Sackville-West. Their deep friendship survived the fading of their three-year love affair, and lasted until Woolf's suicide in 1941. Woolf's novel *Orlando*, about a marvellous, androgynous, immortal character, was an extended love letter to Sackville-West.

March 16th, 1926.

Style is a very simple matter; it is all rhythm. Once you get that, you can't use the wrong words. But on the other hand here am I sitting after half the morning, crammed with ideas, and visions, and so on, and can't dislodge them, for lack of the right rhythm. Now this is very profound, what rhythm is, and goes far deeper than words. A sight, an emotion, creates this wave in the mind, long

120

before it makes words to fit it; and in writing (such is my present belief) one has to recapture this, and set this working (which has nothing apparently to do with words) and then, as it breaks and tumbles in the mind, it makes words to fit it.

September 8th, 1928.

I believe that the main thing in beginning a novel is to feel, not that you can write it, but that it exists on the far side of a gulf, which words can't cross: that it's to be pulled through only in a breathless anguish. Now when I sit down to an article, I have a net of words which will come down on the idea certainly in an hour or so. But a novel, as I say, to be good should seem, before one writes it, something unwriteable: but only visible; so that for nine months one lives in despair, and only when one has forgotten what one meant, does the book seem tolerable. I assure you, all my novels were first rate before they were written.

...

Alexander Woollcott

Alexander Woollcott (1887—1943), American playwright, journalist and critic, wrote this paean of praise to American film producer Walt Disney on January 12th, 1942.

After seeing *Dumbo* for the third time, I suspect that if we could get far enough away to see it in its place, we would recognize it as the highest achievement yet achieved in the Seven Arts since the first white man landed on this continent. This cautious tribute is paid by one who was several degrees short of nuts about *Snow White* and a little bored by *Pinocchio* ... But *Dumbo* is that once far-off divine event toward which your whole creation has moved.

After some thought, I have decided you are the most valuable person alive, so for God's sake take care of yourself.

...

Edith Sitwell

Edith Sitwell (1887—1964), English writer and poet, wrote this letter to Charlotte Franken Haldane, English novelist, biographer and autobiographer, on December 5th, 1933.

I love Bach, too. But though I admire Mozart, I love him less, which is my fault, preferring infinitely, Gluck, because he is less sweet. Bach is my god. He seems to have created a perfect world, in which there is no sin, and in which sorrow is holy and not ugly.

Sir Laurence Olivier

This telegram was despatched by Sir Laurence Olivier (1907—89), English actor, producer and director, to English playwright Christopher Fry on October 29th, 1949. Fry had been sending his play *Venus Observed* to Olivier in instalments.

DEAR FELLOW ACT ONE PROVOCATIVE SO EXHILARATING SO DELICIOUS CANNOT RESIST WITHHOLDING MYSELF IN TINGLING RESISTANCE FROM THE JOYS OF ACT TWO BY PAUSING TO SEND YOU THIS WIRE WITH LOVE LARRY

...

Kenneth Tynan

Kenneth Tynan (1927—80), English journalist and critic, wrote this silver-tongued tribute to American television host Johnny Carson on April 22nd, 1979. Tynan was the creator of the controversial show *Oh, Calcutta*. He also worked for a time with Sir Laurence Olivier at the National Theatre, taking the role of literary manager.

When I read in the paper that you might be quitting *The Tonight Show* in the fall, I felt a twinge of quite definite grief, and suddenly realized how much it meant to me, when contemplating a trip to this country, to reflect that whatever else might have dried up or degenerated, one sparkling fountainhead of pleasure would still remain — Carson at 11:30 ... I hear ... that you are bored. Was Dickens bored after writing novels for seventeen years? Did Matisse burn his brushes after seventeen years' daubing? ... We all know that you are like a great dish that combines all your flavours. It resembles the pressed duck at the Tour d'Argent in Paris: the recipe hasn't changed in my lifetime, yet it tastes as inimitably fresh every time I order it.

Was it unadventurous for Astaire to stick to tap-dancing instead of venturing into ballet? On the contrary: it was brave, and it was what made him (and will keep him forever) a classic. Similarly, I honour Cary Grant for never having played *Macbeth* and Muhammad Ali for keeping out of the Wimbledon championships.

History

...a letter always feels to me like immortality because it is the mind alone without a corporeal friend.

Emily Dickinson, (1830—86)
American poet

Marcus Tullius Cicero

Marcus Tullius Cicero (106—43 BC) was a Roman orator, writer and statesman, whose letters provide a picture of life in ancient Rome. He wrote to his friend, Atticus, in December 44 BC, describing a visit from Julius Caesar.

Well, I have no reason after all to repent my formidable guest! For he made himself exceedingly pleasant. But on his arrival at the villa of Philippus on the evening of the second day of the Saturnalia, the villa was so choke full of soldiers that there was scarcely a dining-room left for Caesar himself to dine in. Two thousand men, if you please! I was in a great taking as to what was to happen the next day; and so Cassius Barba came to my aid and gave me guards. A camp was pitched in the open, the villa was put in a state of defence. He stayed with Philippus on the third day of the Saturnalia till one o'clock, without admitting anyone. He was engaged on his accounts, I think, with Balbus. Then he took a walk on the beach. After two he went to the bath … He was anointed: took his place at the table. He was under a course of emetics, and so ate and drank without scruple and as suited his taste. It was a very good dinner … Besides this, the staff were entertained in three rooms in a very liberal style. The freedom of lower rank and the slaves had everything they could want. But the upper sort had a really recherché dinner. In fact, I showed that I was somebody. However, he is not a guest to whom one would say, 'Pray look me up again on your way back.' Once is enough. We didn't say a word about politics. There was plenty of literary talk. In short, he was pleased and enjoyed himself. He said he should stay one day at Puteoli, another at Baiae. That's the story of the entertainment, or I might call it the billeting on me — trying to the temper, but not seriously inconvenient. I am staying on here for a short time and then go to Tusculum. When he was passing Dolabella's villa, the whole guard formed up on the right and left of his horse, and nowhere else. This I was told by Nicias.

…

Saint Paul the Apostle

Saint Paul the Apostle (c. 10—c. 65 AD), then known as Saul, was active in the persecution of Christians until he experienced a vision of Christ on the road to Damascus and was converted. He became one of the first great Christian missionaries. In a series of famous letters, *The Epistles*, he laid out his beliefs for the Christian church in Corinth. This extract is from his *1st Epistle to the Corinthians*, AD 56.

Unto the Church of God which is at Corinth, to them that are sanctified in Christ Jesus, called to be saints, with all that in every place call upon the name of Jesus Christ our Lord, both theirs and ours:

Now I beseech you, brethren, by the name of our Lord Jesus Christ, that ye all speak the same thing, and that there be no divisions among you; but that ye be perfectly joined together in the same mind and in the same judgement ...

Now concerning the things whereof ye wrote unto me: it is good for a man not to touch a woman. Nevertheless, to avoid fornication, let every man have his own wife, and let every woman have her own husband. Let the husband render unto the wife due benevolence: and likewise also the wife unto the husband. The wife hath not power of her own body, but the husband: and likewise also the husband hath not power of his own body, but the wife. Defraud ye not one the other, except it be with consent for a time, that ye may give yourselves to fasting and prayer; and come together again, that Satan tempt you not for your incontinency.

But I speak this by permission, and not of commandment. For I would that all men were even as I myself. But every man hath his proper gift of God, one after this manner, and another after that.

I say therefore to the unmarried and widows, it is good for them if they abide even as I. But if they cannot contain, let them marry: for it is better to marry than to burn.

And unto the married I command, yet not I, but the Lord, let not the wife depart from her husband: but and if she depart, let her remain unmarried, or be reconciled to her husband; and let not the husband put away his wife ...

When I was a child, I spoke as a child, I understood as a child, I thought as a child: but when I became a man, I put away childish things.

For now we see through a glass, darkly; but then face to face: now I know in part; but then shall I know even as also I am known. And now abideth faith, hope, charity, these three; but the greatest of these is charity ... My love be with you all in Christ Jesus. Amen.

...

Pliny the Younger

Pliny the Younger (62—113 AD), Roman lawyer and scholar, wrote to his friend, Tacitus, describing the death of his Uncle, Pliny the Elder, during the eruption of Vesuvius in AD 79.

My uncle died in a disaster that struck one of the most lovely parts of the world. ...

My uncle was in charge of the Roman fleet at Misenum. About

two o'clock on August 24th my mother showed me a cloud which was very big and looked odd. My uncle ... called a slave to fetch his shoes, climbed up a hill and got the best view he could of the mystery.

The cloud was getting bigger and it had a flat head, like a Mediterranean Pine tree. It was carried up into the air on a very long trunk which broke into branches. The trunk was made by the blast from the volcano pushing up hard. As it got higher into the atmosphere, the blast was less strong and the ash got heavier and began to fan out. The cloud sometimes glowed white hot, sometimes the earth and ash in it made it dirty and blotchy. For a long time we did not know which mountain it was coming from. It was only later we found it was Vesuvius.

My uncle, who was a great scholar, just could not keep away ... He ordered all the warships to be launched and he went on one himself. ... He sailed right into the middle of the danger ... When they got near Pompeii, the ashes were hotter and fell more thickly. They were also hit by pumice and stones. These had been burned black and broken into pieces by the fires. All of a sudden they sailed into the shallows, which were full of debris from the volcano. For a moment my uncle stopped and thought he might turn back. When the helmsman said he should, he replied, 'Fortune favours the fearless. Sail round to the villa of Pomponianus!' ...

The wind helped my uncle's ship to get there very quickly ... While they were having their dinner, huge sheets of flame shot up all over the place and great walls of fire flashed in answer to them. When it got dark, the fire and flames seemed brighter than ever. ... By now the houses were shaking with the huge tremors. These were coming thick and fast. Buildings were being torn from their foundations and seemed to sway backwards and forwards. If my uncle and his friend went outside, they felt they would be hurt by falling pumice, even though this was light and hollow ...

My uncle decided to go out onto the shore and see for himself if the sea would let them sail. But it was still angry and against them ... Then the flames and the smell of sulphur, which always tells you the flames are coming, made the others run away. These flames made him wake up. He stood up, leaning on two young slaves, but he fell down straight away. I suppose the thick fumes had blocked his windpipe and closed his gullet which was always weak and giving him trouble. When they found his body in the light two days later, there was not a mark on it. ... He looked like a man who was having a rest, not a man who had died ... I have put down in full everything I had a part in and everything I heard at the time. I have done this very carefully ... It is one thing to write a letter. It is another thing to write history. It is one thing to write for a friend. It is another thing to write for the world.

...

Kuyuk Khan

Kuyuk Khan (1206—48) was the grandson of the great chief Genghis Khan who established the mighty Mongol Empire in the twelfth century. Genghis was succeeded by his son Ogatai and then in 1246 by Kuyuk. This was Kuyuk Khan's reply to a letter from Pope Innocent IV, in which he had threatened him with the wrath of God if he continued to persecute Christians.

By the power of the Eternal Heaven, We are the all-embracing Khan of the United Great Nations. It is our command:

This is a decree, sent to the great Pope that he may know and pay heed.

After holding counsel with the monarchs under your suzerainty, you have sent us an offer of subordination, which we have accepted from the hands of your envoy.

If you should act up to your word, then you, the great Pope, should come in person with the monarchs to pay us homage ...

Furthermore, you have said it would be well for us to become Christians. You write to me in person about this matter, and have addressed to me a request. This, your request, we cannot understand.

Furthermore, you have written me these words: 'You have attacked all the territories of the Magyars and other Christians, at which I am astonished. Tell me, what was their crime?' These your words, we likewise cannot understand. Genghis Khan and Ogatai Khan revealed the commands of Heaven ... Those of whom you speak showed themselves highly presumptuous and slew our envoys. Therefore, in accordance with the commands of the Eternal Heaven the inhabitants of the aforesaid countries have been slain and annihilated. If not by the command of Heaven, how can anyone slay or conquer out of his own strength?

And when you say: 'I am a Christian. I pray to God. I arraign and despise others,' how do you know who is pleasing to God, and to whom He allots His grace? How can you know it, that you speak such words?

Thanks to the power of the Eternal Heaven, all lands have been given to us from sunrise to sunset. How could anyone act other than in accordance with the commands of Heaven? Now your own upright heart must tell you: 'We will become subject to you, and will place our powers at your disposal.' You in person, at the head of monarchs, all of you, without exception, must come to tender us service and pay us homage, then only will we recognize your submission. But if you do not obey the commands of Heaven, and run counter to our orders, we shall know that you are our foe.

That is what we have to tell you. If you fail to act in accordance therewith, how can we foresee what will happen to you? Heaven alone knows.

...

Dante Alighieri

Dante Alighieri (1265—1321), the famous Italian poet, spent the last twenty years of his life exiled from his native Florence because his political opinions did not accord with those in power. This letter, written in 1316 to a friend whom he addressed as father, probably as a sign of respect, shows how he responded to his supporters' attempts to gain him pardon.

From your letter, which I received with due respect and affection, and have diligently studied, I learn with gratitude how my recall to Florence has been the object of your care and concern; and I am the more beholden to you therefore, inasmuch as it rarely happens that an exile finds friends. My reply to what you have written, although perchance it be not of such tenor as certain faint hearts would desire, I earnestly beg may be carefully examined and considered by you before judgement be passed upon it.

I gather ... I may receive pardon, and be permitted to return forthwith, on condition that I pay a certain sum of money, and submit to the stigma of the oblation — two propositions, my father, which in sooth are as ridiculous as they are ill advised — This, then, is the gracious recall of Dante Alighieri to his native city, after the miseries of well-nigh fifteen years of exile! ...

No! my father, not by this path will I return to my native city. If some other can be found ... which does not derogate from the fame and honour of Dante, that will I tread with no lagging steps. But if by no such path Florence may be entered, then will I enter Florence never. What! Can I not anywhere gaze upon the face of the sun and the stars? Can I not under any sky contemplate the most precious truths, without first returning to Florence, disgraced, nay dishonoured, in the eyes of my fellow citizens? Assuredly bread will not fail me!

...

Francesco Petrarca

Francesco Petrarca (1304—74), Italian poet, wrote to his friend Socrates on the evils of the world and the plague (Black Death), which had devastated Europe. The letter is dated June 11th, 1351.

What shall I do first? Shall I voice my laments or my fears? Everywhere there is cause for grief; and all present woes give promise of deeper woes to come. And yet, I can scarcely conceive what worse evils can possibly be expected. The world has been destroyed and brought to an end by the madness of men and by the avenging hand of God. We have sunk to such depths of misery that no new species of misfortune occurs to the mind. Whosoever, indeed, will narrate the present state of humanity to posterity — provided any descendants survive us — will seem to be recounting mere fables. Nor will it be right to wax indignant if we should be given less credence in matters which we ourselves would not believe from others. As for myself, I frankly confess that the present times, in which mankind has experienced every conceivable evil, have made me more prone to believe many things of which I had been sceptical.

I shall pass over those floods and hurricanes and conflagrations, whereby cities that were flourishing one moment perished root and branch the next. I shall pass over, too, those wars raging throughout the world and attended by endless slaughter of men. I shall touch but lightly, furthermore, upon this heaven-sent plague, unheard of during the ages. They are matters well known to all. The depopulated cities and fields deprived of their tillers bear witness to them; the face of the earth, afflicted and well-nigh turned into a desert — aye Nature herself, so to speak — sheds tears of sorrow ...

...

King Henry V of England

Henry V (1387—1422) was King of England from 1413. This was his proclamation to his soldiers before the Battle of Agincourt, October 24th, 1415 — St Crispin's Day — when his army defeated the French.

So it is, my valiant Englishmen! We must either conquer or die, for victory or death is all the present prospect! But death is the least you can suffer, if you be not victorious. No: you are to expect lingering tortures, and the most vile, inhumane usage, from a barbarous enemy, who are so cruel, that your lives cannot satiate their rage; but they have threatened to cut off the thumbs of every one of you, archers, that you may forever be disabled to draw a bow against them. We must, therefore, fight with a resolution undaunted and invincible. And why should we fear death, or be doubtful of victory, since God, who guards our lives, has given us courage to defend them, and will strengthen us to conquer? ...

Therefore, though I have great confidence in your valour yet that is the least part of my hopes — 'tis the assistance of the Almighty which gives me the firmest assurance of victory. And, that the same religious confidence may be excited in your souls, know that, by a remarkable working of divine providence, our enemies offer us battle on the day which has been appointed in England for the people to implore a blessing on our arms. Know that, while you are fighting, your fathers, your wives, and your children, with lifted eyes and hands, and bended knees, are supplicating the favour of heaven for your safety and success ... Proceed we then, my brave countrymen, with confidence in God, and with all hopes that valiant men, resolved to conquer or die, may have in their arms. Let us charge them, in a firm persuasion of victory — victory! ...

...

Joan of Arc

Joan of Arc (1412—31) dictated this letter demanding the surrender of the English army, which was besieging the town of Orleans in 1429. This document was later used against her at her trial for heresy in which she was sentenced to death. Charles, 'the true heir' referred to in the text, was the Dauphin, who became Charles VII after Joan persuaded him to be crowned at Reims in the same year.

King of England, and you, Duke of Bedford, who call yourself Regent of the realm of France, you William de la Pole, Earl of Suffolk, John Talbot, and you, Thomas, Lord Scales, who call yourselves lieutenants of the said Bedford —

Submit to the King of Heaven; surrender to the Maid who has been sent by God the keys of all the good cities which you have taken and violated in France. She has come by God's order to restore the royal blood. She is ready to make peace, if you will submit, provided that you quit France and pay for what you have taken. And you, archers, gentlemen, soldiers of whatever rank before Orléans, depart in God's name into your own country; and if you will not, expect soon to see the Maid, who will inflict great damage upon you.

King of England, if you fail to do as I ask, I am a military chieftain and, in whatever place in France I come upon your men, I shall cause them to depart, whether by their will or no; and if they refuse to obey I shall have them killed. I am sent here by God the King of Heaven to meet them body to body and drive them out of the realm of France. But if they will yield I will grant them mercy. And doubt it not, for you shall not have the realm of France from God, the King of Heaven, son of Saint Mary, but it will be held by Charles, the true heir, for God wishes it and has so revealed to him by the Maid, and he will enter Paris with a noble company.

If you will not believe the tidings sent you from God and the

Maid, we shall strike you down in whatever place we find you, and make you such a great 'hahay' as has not been seen in France for a thousand years unless you submit to us. And know well that God will lend such strength to the Maid that you will be unable to withstand her and her good soldiers ...

...

Christopher Columbus

Christopher Columbus (1451—1506) was Italian by birth, but was commissioned to make his voyage of discovery by the Spanish monarchs, Isabel and Ferdinand. He set sail from Spain with three ships, the *Santa Maria*, the *Pinta* and the *Niña*, and reached land, an island off the coast of America, on October 12th, 1492. On March 14th, 1493, he wrote this letter to Gabriel Sánchez, Treasurer of King Ferdinand of Spain, describing his discoveries.

Because my undertakings have attained success, I know that it will be pleasing to you: these I have determined to relate, so that you may be made acquainted with everything done and discovered in this our voyage. On the thirty-third day after I departed from Cadiz, I came to the Indian sea, where I found many islands inhabited by men without number, all of which I took possession for our most fortunate king, with proclaiming heralds and flying standards, no one objecting.

To the first of these I gave the name of the blessed Saviour, on whose aid relying I had reached this as well as the other islands. But the Indians called it Guanahany. I also called each one of the others by a new name. For I ordered one island to be called Santa Maria of the Conception, another Fernandina, another Isabella, another Juana, and so on with the rest ...

In all these islands there is no difference in the appearance of the people, nor in the manners and language, but all understand each other mutually; a fact that is very important for the end which I suppose to be earnestly desired by our most illustrious king, that is, their conversion to the holy religion of Christ, to which in truth, as far as I can perceive, they are ready and favourably inclined ...

If anyone has written or said anything about these islands, it was all with obscurities and conjectures; no one claims that he had seen them; from which they seemed like fables. Therefore let the king and queen, the princes and their most fortunate kingdoms, and all other countries of Christendom give thanks to our Lord and Saviour Jesus Christ, who has bestowed upon us so great a victory and gift. Let religious processions be solemnized; let sacred festivals be given; let the churches be covered with festive garlands. Let Christ rejoice on earth, as he rejoices in heaven, when he foresees coming to salvation so many souls of people hitherto lost. Let us be glad also, as well on account of the exaltation of our faith, as on account of the increase of our temporal affairs, of which not only Spain, but universal Christendom will be partaker ...

...

King Henry VII of England

Henry VII (1457—1509) spent his early life abroad, returning in 1485 to lead a rebellion against Richard III, which ended with the death of Richard at the Battle of Bosworth and the accession of Henry to the throne of England. On July 17th, 1497, he wrote to his mother, Margaret Beaufort, who had given birth to him before she was fourteen and supported him for nearly 30 years in his claim to the throne.

Madam, my most entirely well-beloved lady and mother, I recommend me unto you in the most humble and lowly wise that I can, beseeching you of your daily and continual blessings. By your confessor, the bearer, I have received your good and most loving writing, and by the same have heard at good leisure such credence as he would show unto me on your behalf, and thereupon has sped him in every behalf, without delay, according to your noble petition and desire ... And my dame, not only in this but in all other things that I may know should be to your honour, and pleasure, and weal of your soul, I shall be as glad to please you as your heart can desire it, and I know well, that I am as much bounden so to do, as any creature living, for the great and singular motherly love and affection it hath pleased you at all times to bear towards me. Wherefore, my own most loving mother, in my most hearty manner I thank you, beseeching you of your good continuance in the same.

...

Vasco da Gama

Vasco da Gama (1460—1524), the Portuguese navigator, was sent by the King and Queen of Portugal to discover the route to India. He reached land on Christmas Day 1497 and named it Natal, then continued across the Indian Ocean to Calicut, becoming the first man to link Europe with the East. Dom Manuel, King of Portugal, wrote to the Catholic monarchs of Spain in July 1499, announcing the discovery.

Very high, most excellent Princes and most powerful lords. Your Highnesses know how we had sent out to discover Vasco da Gama, *fidalgo* of our household, and with him his brother Paulo da Gama, with four ships through the ocean, who had been gone for about two years now; and as the principal purpose of this enterprise for our predecessors had always been the service of God and our profit, He in His Mercy decided to bring it about, according to a message that we have had from one of the captains who has now returned to us in this city, so that India and other neighbouring Kingdoms and Seignories have been found and discovered; and they entered and navigated her [India's] sea in which they found great cities and great edifices and rivers and great settlements, in which is conducted all the trade in spices and stones that passes in ships, which the same discoverers saw and found in great quantities, and of great size, to Meca, and from there to Cairo, from where it spreads out throughout the world.

...

Hernando Cortés

Hernando Cortés (1485—1547) was the first of the Spanish conquistadors who set out to find fame and fortune in South America and conquer it for the Spanish crown. He overthrew the Aztec Empire (1519—21) and claimed Mexico (Yucatan) for Spain. This letter, which Cortés claimed to be the first true account of the discoveries, was sent to Queen Doña Juana and her son, the Emperor Charles V, by the Justiciary and Municipal Council of the Muy Rica Villa de Vera Cruz on July 10th, 1519.

Most high, mighty and excellent Princes, most Catholic and powerful Kings and Sovereigns:

We have reason to believe that Your Royal Highnesses have been informed, by the letters of Diego Velázquez, the admiral's lieutenant in the island of Fernandina [Cuba], of a new land that was discovered in these parts some two years ago more or less, and which was first called Cozumel and later Yucatan, without it being either the one or the other as Your Royal Highnesses shall see from our report. For the accounts previously made of this land to Your Majesties, as to its wealth, and the way in which it was discovered and other details which have been described, were not, nor could have been true, as in this report we are sending Your Majesties, because until now no one has known any of these things. Here we will treat of the beginning, when it was first discovered, up until its present state, so that Your Highnesses may know what land it is, what people live in it, the way in which they live, their rites and ceremonies, religions and customs and what profit Your Highnesses may gain from it, or have already gained; and by whom Your Majesties have been served, so that Your Highnesses may in all things do as You see fit.

Thomas More

Thomas More (1478—1535) was a statesman and author, originally much favoured by Henry VIII, and made Lord Chancellor in 1529. He fell from grace for refusing to acknowledge the King as head of the church after Henry had broken away from the Pope and the church of Rome in order to marry Anne Boleyn. This letter was sent to his daughter, Margaret Roper, on the eve of his execution, July 6th, 1535.

Mine own good daughter, our Lord be thanked, I am in good health of body, and in good quiet of mind; and of worldly things I no more desire than I have. I beseech Him make you all merry in the hope of heaven. And such things as I somewhat longed to talk with you all, concerning the world to come, our Lord put them into your minds, as I trust He doth, and better too, by His holy spirit; who bless you and preserve you all. Written with a coal by your tender loving father, who in his poor prayers forgetteth none of you all, nor your babes, nor your nurses, nor your husbands, nor your good husbands' shrewd wives, nor your father's shrewd wife neither, nor our other friends. And thus fare ye heartily well ...

...

Mary, Queen of Scots

Mary Queen of Scots (1542—87) was the daughter of James V of Scotland. She married the Dauphin of France at the age of sixteen. Widowed at nineteen, Mary returned in 1561 as Queen of Scotland, but unwise marriages and intrigues led to her abdication and exile in England. Accused of conspiring against Elizabeth I, she was executed on February 8th, 1587. This was her last letter to her brother, the Earl of Moray, written in the early hours of the morning of her execution.

Sir, my good brother, having under God's hand for my sins, as I believe, come to throw me in the arms of this Queen, my cousin, where I have had much trouble and passed nigh twenty years, I am at last by her and her Estates condemned to death, and having claimed my papers, by them confiscated, to the end of making my testament, I have been unable to recover aught that would serve me, nor to gain leave freely to make the same, nor that after my death my body should be transported, as I desire, into your realm, where I have had the honour to be queen, your sister and ancient ally.

This day and afternoon has been pronounced to me my sentence, to be executed tomorrow as a criminal, at eight o'clock of the morning. I have not had leisure to make you a full discourse of all that has passed, but if it please you to credit my doctor and those others, my heart-broken servants, you will hear the truth; and as, God be thanked, I despise death and in good faith protest that I receive it innocent of all crime ...

This Wednesday, at two hours after midnight.

Your most loving and very good sister,

Mari R.

...

Queen Elizabeth I of England

Queen Elizabeth I (1533—1603) wrote to James VI of Scotland after the beheading of his mother, Mary, Queen of Scots. In this letter, written on February 14th, 1587, Elizabeth assured him of her innocence of any responsibility for the fate that had befallen his mother.

My dear brother:

I would you knew (though not felt) the extreme dolour that overwhelms my mind, for that miserable accident which (far contrary to my meaning) hath befallen. I have now sent this kinsman of mine, whom by now it has pleased you to favour, to instruct you truly of that which is too irksome for my pen to tell you. I beseech you, as God and many more know, how innocent I am in this case; so you will believe me, that if I had bid ought I would have bid by it. I am not so base-minded that fear of any living creature or prince should make me afraid to do that were just; or done, to deny the same. I am not of so base a lineage, nor carry so vile a mind. But, as not to disguise fits not a king, so will I never dissemble my actions, but cause them show even as I meant them. Thus assuring yourself of me, that as I know this was deserved, yet if I had meant it I would never lay it on others' shoulder; no more will I not damnify myself that thought it not. The circumstance it may please you to have of this bearer. And for your part, think you have not in the world a more loving kinswoman, nor a more dear friend than myself; nor any that will watch more carefully to preserve you and your estate. And who shall otherwise persuade you, judge them more partial to others than you. And thus in haste I leave to trouble you: beseeching God to send you a long reign.

Your most assured loving sister and cousin,

Elizab. R.

...

Robert Devereux

Robert Devereux, second Earl of Essex (1566—1601) was a soldier and politician who became the favourite of Elizabeth I from 1587, when he was 21 and the Queen was 54. He fell from favour and was banished from court and finally executed in 1601. He sent this letter to the Queen after his downfall, around 1600.

From a mind delighting in sorrow, from spirits wasted in passion, from a heart torn in pieces with care, grief, and travel, from a man that hateth himself and all things that keepeth him alive, what service can your Majesty expect, since your service past deserves no more than banishment or prescription in the cursedest of all other countries? Nay, nay, it is your rebels' pride and success that must give me leave to ransom my life out of this hateful prison of my loathed body; which if it happen so, your Majesty shall have no cause to mislike the fashion of my death, since the course of my life could never please you. Your Majesty's exiled servant.

...

The Gunpowder Plot

In 1605, the Gunpowder Plot was hatched by a group of Catholic conspirators. Its object was to blow up James I and the members of both Houses of Parliament. This document, warning of impending danger and known as the Monteagle Letter, was delivered anonymously to Lord Monteagle on October 26th that year, and led to the arrest of the plotters in the cellars of the Houses of Parliament.

My Lord, out of the love I bear to some of your friends, I have a care of your preservation. Therefore I would advise you, as you tender your life, to devise some excuse to shift of your attendance at this Parliament; for God and man hath concurred to punish the wickedness of this time. And think not slightly of this advertisement, but retire yourself into your country [county] where you may expect the event in safety. For though there be no appearance of any stir, yet I say they shall receive a terrible blow this Parliament; and yet they shall see not who hurts them. This counsel is not to be condemned because it may do you good and can do you no harm; for the danger is passed as soon as you have burnt the letter. And I hope God will give you the grace to make good use of it, to whose holy protection I commend you.

...

Edward Trelawney

Edward Trelawney was sent out to America as an agent by his brother, Robert, a merchant in Plymouth, England. In 1635 he wrote home to tell of his joy in the new country. Thousands of Puritans emigrated from England to New England in the 1630s, searching for this new beginning.

For my part I have just cause even to bless the Lord for so high a favour in bringing me hither. Oh dear brother, I now find what it is to be a Christian. After many a temptation, many a hard conflict and buffeting with Satan, many a heavy sigh, deep groan, salt and sorrowful tear, I thank God through Jesus Christ our Lord, who hath brought me out of darkness into His glorious light. Oh Newe England, Newe England, how much am I bound to the Lord for granting me so great mercy as to tread on thy grounds. Oh that Old England could but speak in thy language; then would not the holy and heavenly and sacred name of the great and glorious God be so irreverently tossed and tumbled, so profanely torn in pieces in men's mouths; then would not there be so many abominations and wickedness committed in the hearth and houses of thy people, but thou shouldst then be blest and beloved of the Lord as New England is.

And what is the reason of all this? Surely one is (as I conceive) that as God's people are come into a new country, where they may freely enjoy the liberty of his holy ordinance without any trouble or molestation at all, either of bishop, archbishop, or any other inferior carping minister or gaping officer, so they come unto the land and to the Lord with new hearts and new lives, and enter into a new covenant.

...

Cotton Mather

Cotton Mather (1663—1728) was a Puritan minister in Boston, New England. He came from a prominent Puritan family and wrote many books on theology, history and science. He defended the Salem witch trials and was strongly prejudiced against Quakers, as can be seen from the following letter to his old friend, John Higginson, in which he refers to William Penn, the Quaker founder of Pennsylvania, as 'the chief scamp'.

There be now at sea a ship called *Welcome*, which has on board 100 or more of the heretics and malignants called Quakers, with W Penn, who is the chief scamp, at the head of them. The General Court has accordingly given sacred orders to Master Malachi Huscott, of the brig Porpoise, to waylay the said *Welcome* slyly as near the Cape of Cod as may be, and make captive the said Penn and his ungodly crew, so that the Lord may be glorified and not mocked on the soil of this new country with the heathen worship of these people. Much spoil can be made of selling the whole lot to Barbados, where slaves fetch good prices in rum and sugar, and we shall not only do the Lord great good by punishing the wicked, but we shall make great good for His Minister and people.

Yours in the bowels of Christ,
Cotton Mather

...

Oliver Cromwell

Oliver Cromwell (1599—1658), English general and politician, was the Puritan leader of the parliamentary side (the Roundheads) in the Civil War against the Royalists (1642—51), which overthrew King Charles I and led to his execution in 1649. Cromwell ruled as Lord Protector from 1653 until his death. This letter was written by Cromwell to the speaker of the House of Commons, William Lenthall, on June 14th, 1645, the day of the Battle of Naseby, the decisive confrontation of the Civil War when the Royalists were defeated.

Haverbrowe

Sir,
Being commanded by you to this service, I think my self bound to acquaint you with the good hand of God towards you and us. We marched yesterday after the King, who went before us from Daventree to Havebrowe, and quartered about six miles from him. This day we marched towards him. He drew out to meet us; both armies engaged; we after 3 hours fight, very doubtful, at last routed his army, killed and took about 5000, very many officers, but of what quality we yet know not. We took also about 200 carriages, all he had, and all his guns, being 12 in number, whereof 2 were demi-cannon, 2 demi-culverins, and (I think) the rest sakers. We pursued the enemy from three miles short of Haverbrowe to nine beyond, even to sight of Leicester, whether the King fled. Sir, this is none other but the hand of God, and to him alone belongs the glory, wherein none are to share with him. The General served you with all faithfullness and honour, and the best commendations I can give him is that I dare say he attributes all to God, and would rather perish than assume to himself, which is an honest and a thriving way, and yet as much for bravery may be given to him in this action as to a man. Honest men served you faithfully in this action. Sir, they are trusty; I beseech you in the name of God not to discourage them. I wish this action may beget thankfullness and humility in all that are concerned in it. He that ventures his life for the liberty of his country, I wish he trust God

for the liberty of his conscience and you for the liberty he fights for.
In this he rests who is
　　Your most humble servant,
　　　Oliver Cromwell

...

King Charles II of England

Charles II (1630—85) was the son of Charles I, who had been executed at the time
of the Civil War when the monarchy was abolished. On the death of the Lord
Protector, Oliver Cromwell, the Restoration Party sought the return of the
monarchy. In this letter to General Monck, the exiled Charles announced his
decision to return to England. Monck was leader of the Restoration Party, and had
been authorized to petition Charles to return to the throne. Charles became king in
1660 and ruled until his death.

If this be the first letter you have received from me, it is only
because some of your friends have not found a convenience of
delivering one to you, which they have had long in their hands. And
you cannot but believe that I know too well the power you have to
do me good or harm, not to desire you should be my friend. And I
think I have the best ground of confidence that can be that you will
be so, in believing you to be a great lover of your country and that
you desire to secure the peace and happiness and to advance the
honour of it, and knowing very well that my heart is full of no other
end, which I am sure you will know yourself as soon as you know
me. And whatever you have heard to the contrary, you will find to
be as false as if you had been told that I have white hair or am
crooked. And it is upon this confidence only that I depend upon you
and your assistance to the bringing that to pass which I may say
can only with God's blessing bring peace and happiness to the
nation and restore it to its just reputation and honour, and secure
all good men in the possession of what belongs to them. As I know
these ends can only prevail with you, so I do not think you will be
the less zealous for them, because together with them you advance
my interest and oblige me, who can never be without that sense of
your prince, as the greatness of the obligation merits, and I should
enlarge upon that particular, if I did think it would be acceptable to
you. However, I cannot but say, that I will take all the ways I can,
to let the world see, and you and yours find, that I have an entire
trust in you, and as much kindness for you, as can be expressed by
your affectionate friend,
　　Charles R.

...

Samuel Pepys

Samuel Pepys (1633—1703), the famous diarist, wrote to Lady Elizabeth Carteret, wife of the Treasurer of the Navy, at the height of the plague in London. The letter is dated September 4th, 1665.

Dear Madam;
… The absence of the Court and emptiness of the city takes away all occasion of news, save only such melancholy stories as would rather sadden than find your Ladyship any divertisement in the hearing; I having stayed in the city till above 7400 died in one week, and of them above 6000 of the plague, and little noise heard day nor night but tolling of bells; till I could walk Lumberstreet and not meet twenty persons from one end to the other, and not fifty upon the Exchange; till whole families (ten and twelve together) have been swept away; till my very physician, Dr Burnet, who undertook to secure me against any infection (having survived the month of his own being shut up) died himself of the plague; till the nights (though much lengthened) are grown too short to conceal the burials of those that died the day before, people being thereby constrained to borrow daylight for that service; lastly, till I could find neither food nor drink safe, the butcheries being everywhere visited, my brewer's house shut up, and my baker with his whole family dead of the plague.

Yet, Madam, through God's blessing and the good humours begot in my attendance upon our late Amours, your poor servant is in a perfect state of health, as well as resolution of employing it as your Ladyship and family shall find work for it.

...

Abigail Adams

Abigail Adams (1744—1818) was the wife of John Adams, who would become second President of the United States, after George Washington. Frequently separated from her husband because of the Revolution, she wrote numerous letters to him, giving valuable insights into the upheavals of the times. This letter was written on March 31st, 1776.

I wish you would ever write me a Letter half as long as I write you; and tell me if you may where your Fleet are gone? What sort of Defence Virginia can make against our common Enemy? …

I have sometimes been ready to think that the passion for Liberty cannot be Equally Strong in the Breasts of those who have been accustomed to deprive their fellow Creatures of theirs. Of this I am certain that it is not founded upon that generous and christian principal of doing to others as we would that others should do unto us …

I feel very differently at the approach of spring to what I did a month ago. We knew not then whether we could plant or sow with safety, whether when we had toiled we could reap the fruits of our own industry, whether we could rest in our own Cottages, or whether we should not be driven from the sea coasts to seek shelter in the wilderness, but now we feel as if we might sit under our own vine and eat the good of the land.

I feel a gaiety de Coar to which before I was a stranger. I think the Sun looks brighter, the Birds sing more melodiously, and Nature puts on a more cheerful countenance. We feel a temporary peace, and the poor fugitives are returning to their deserted habitations ... I long to hear that you have declared an independency — and by the way in the new Code of Laws which I suppose it will be necessary for you to make I desire you would Remember the Ladies, and be more generous and favourable to them than your ancestors. Do not put such unlimited power into the hands of the Husbands. Remember all Men would be tyrants if they could. If particular care and attention is not paid to the Ladies we are determined to foment a Rebellion, and will not hold ourselves bound by any Laws in which we have no voice, or Representation.

That your Sex are Naturally Tyrannical is a Truth so thoroughly established as to admit of no dispute, but such of you as wish to be happy willingly give up the harsh title of Master for the more tender and endearing one of Friend. Why then, not put it out of the power of the vicious and the Lawless to use us with cruelty and indignity with impunity. Men of Sense in all Ages abhor those customs which treat us only as the vassals of your Sex. Regard us then as Beings placed by providence under your protection and in imitation of the Supreme Being make use of that power only for our happiness.

...

Benjamin Franklin

Benjamin Franklin (1706—90) was an American author, scientist and statesman, who assisted in the drafting of the Declaration of Independence. From 1776 until 1785, he was ambassador to France, from where he wrote this letter dated March 5th, 1780 to George Washington, the first President of the United States.

Sir,

I received but lately the Letter your Excellency did me the honour of writing to me ... Should Peace arrive after another Campaign or two, and afford us a little Leisure, I should be happy to see your Excellency in Europe, and to accompany you, if my Age and Strength would permit, in visiting some of its ancient and most famous Kingdoms. You would on this Side the Sea, enjoy the great Reputation you have acquir'd, pure and free from those little Shades that the Jealousy and Envy of a Man's Countrymen and Contemporaries are ever endeavouring to cast over living Merit. Here you would know, and enjoy, what Posterity will say of Washington. For a 1000 Leagues have nearly the same Effect with 1000 Years. The feeble Voice of these groveling Passions cannot extend so far either in Time or Distance. At present I enjoy that Pleasure for you: as I frequently hear the old Generals of this martial Country, (who study the Maps of America, and mark upon them all your Operations) speak with sincere Approbation and great Applause of your Conduct, and join in giving you the Character of one of the greatest Captains of the Age.

I must soon quit the Scene, but you may live to see our Country flourish, as it will amazingly and rapidly after the War is over. Like a Field of young Indian Corn, which long Fair weather and Sunshine had enfeebled and discolour'd, and which in that weak State, by a Thunder Gust of violent Wind, Hail and Rain seem'd to be threatened with absolute Destruction; yet the storm being once past, it recovers fresh Verdure, shoots up with double Vigour, and delights the Eye not of its Owner only, but of every observing Traveller.

The best Wishes that can be form'd, for your Health Honour and Happiness, ever attend you, from

Your Excellency's most obedient
and most humble Servant
B.F[ranklin]

...

Marie-Antoinette

Marie-Antoinette (1755—93) was Queen of France from 1774. She was the daughter of Empress Maria Theresa of Austria and married Louis XVI of France in 1770. Her incredible extravagances were deemed to be partly responsible for the French Revolution (1789—92). This letter from Marie-Antoinette to her sister-in-law, Élisabeth, was written on October 16th, 1793, the day of her execution. Her husband had been guillotined in the spring of the same year.

To you, dear sister, I write for the last time. I have just been condemned, not to a disgraceful death, fit for criminals — but to meet your brother again. As innocent as he was, I hope to be like him in his last moments. I am quiet, as one should be if one's conscience does not reproach one. I regret deeply leaving my poor children. You know that I lived only for them and for you, my good, affectionate sister. You, who have sacrificed everything for friendship's sake, in order to remain with us — in what a position do I leave you! During the trial I learned that my daughter has been separated from you. Alas, the poor child! I dare not write to her, she would not receive my letter — I do not even know if this one will reach you. Herewith receive my blessing for them both. I hope that they will later on, when they are grown up, be united with you and be able to enjoy all your loving care. May they both remember what I have incessantly taught them: that principles and conscientious adherence to one's own duties are the most important basis of life, that the friendship and the confidence which they will show one another, will make them happy ...

I must still entrust my last thoughts to you. I should have liked to have written them down from the beginning of the trial, but, apart from the fact that I was not allowed to write, the trial passed so quickly that I really had no time to do so ... I ask God with all my heart to forgive all my sins which I have committed during my lifetime. I hope that He in His mercy will hear my last prayers as well as those which I have said to Him for a long time, so that my soul may share in His mercy and goodness.

I ask all whom I know and especially you, my dear sister, to forgive all the pain that I have unknowingly caused you. I forgive all my enemies all the evil that I have suffered through them. I say farewell herewith to my aunts and all my brothers and sisters. I had friends. The thought of being separated from them for ever and the knowledge of their grief are among the sorrows which I take with me in my last hour. May they at least know that I thought of them to my last moment.

Farewell, good loving sister! May this letter reach you! Forget me not! I embrace you with all my heart, as well as the poor, dear children! My God, how heartrending it is after all to leave them forever! Farewell, Farewell! I shall now only occupy myself with religious duties. As I am not free in my resolutions they will perhaps bring me a priest, but I declare herewith that I shall not say a single word to him, and that I shall treat him as a complete stranger.

...

Sam

Sam, a young sailor on board the flagship *Royal Sovereign* at the Battle of Trafalgar, wrote to his father telling him of the death of Lord Nelson. The letter is dated October or November 1805.

Honoured Father,

This comes to tell you that I am alive and hearty except three fingers; but that's not much, it might have been my head. I told brother Tom I should like to see a greadly battle, and I have seen one, and we have peppered the Combined rarely (off Trafalgar); and for the matter of that, they fought us pretty tightish for French and Spanish. Three of our mess are killed, and four more of us winged. But to tell you the truth of it, when the game began, I wished myself at Warnborough with my plough again; but when they had given us one duster, and I found myself snug and tight, I set to in good earnest, and thought no more about being killed than if I were at Murrell Green Fair, and I was presently as busy and as black as a collier. How my fingers got knocked overboard I don't know, but off they are, and I never missed them till I wanted them. You see, by my writing, it was my left hand, so I can write to you and fight for my King yet. We have taken a rare parcel of ships, but the wind is so rough we cannot bring them home, else I should roll in money, so we are busy smashing 'em and blowing 'em up wholesale.

Our dear Admiral Nelson is killed! so we have paid pretty sharply for licking 'em. I never set eyes on him, for which I am both sorry and glad; for to be sure, I should like to have seen him — but then, all the men in our ship are such soft toads, they have done nothing but blast their eyes, and cry, ever since he was killed. God bless you! chaps that fought like the devil, sit down and cry like a wench. I am still in the *Royal Sovereign*, but the Admiral has left her, for she is like a horse without a bridle, so he is in a frigate that he may be here and there and everywhere, for he's as *cute* as here and there one, and as bold as a lion, for all he can cry! I saw his tears with my own eyes, when the boat hailed and said my Lord was dead. So no more at present from

Your dutiful Son,
Sam

...

Napoleon Bonaparte

Napoleon Bonaparte (1769—1821), the Corsican general who became Ruler of France after the French Revolution, embarked on a mission to conquer Europe. He was finally defeated and captured by Wellington at the Battle of Waterloo. He wrote to the British Prince Regent (later George IV), asking for protection. The letter was not successful. Napoleon was considered too dangerous to be treated with generosity and was imprisoned for the rest of his life on the remote Atlantic island of St Helena. This letter was written on July 13th, 1815.

Royal Highness:
A victim of the factions which divide my country, and to the enmity of the greatest powers of Europe, I have terminated my political career, and I come, like Themistocles, to throw myself upon the hospitality of the British people. I place myself under the protection of their laws, which I claim of your Royal Highness as the most powerful, the most constant, and the most generous of my enemies.
Napoleon

...

Harriet Beecher Stowe

Harriet Beecher Stowe (1811—96) was an American suffragist and abolitionist. Her famous novel, *Uncle Tom's Cabin*, written and serialized in 1851—2, was influential in the campaign against slavery. These letters between Harriet and her sister, Mrs Edward Beecher, were the spark from which the novel came to life.

Letter from her sister, Mrs Edward Beecher, 1850.

Hattie, if I could use a pen as you can, I would write something to make this whole nation feel what an accursed thing slavery is.

In December, Harriet Beecher Stowe sent this letter to her sister.

Tell Katy I thank her for her letter and will answer it. As long as the baby sleeps with me nights I can't do much at anything, but I will do it at last. I will write that thing if I live.
What are folks in general saying about the slave law, and the stand taken by Boston ministers universally, except Edward? To me it is incredible, amazing, mournful!! I feel as if I should be willing to sink with it, were all this sin and misery to sink in the sea ... I wish father would come on to Boston and preach on the Fugitive Slave Law, as he once preached on the slave-trade, when I was a little girl in Litchfield. I sobbed aloud in one pew and Mrs Judge Reeves in another. I wish some Martin Luther would arise to set this community right.

145

Chief Seattle

Chief Seattle (c. 1784—1866) was Chief of the Dwamish, Suquamish and allied Native American tribes. He ceded his lands in Washington State by the Treaty of Point Elliot in January 1855. He wrote, via an amanuensis, to the American President, Franklin Pierce, in 1854.

How can you buy or sell the sky, the warmth of the land? The idea is strange to us.

If we do not own the freshness of the air and the sparkle of the water, how can you buy them?

Every part of the earth is sacred to my people.

Every shining pine needle, every sandy shore, every mist in the dark woods, every clearing and humming insect is holy in the memory and experience of my people. The sap which courses through the trees carried the memories of the red man.

The white man's dead forget the country of their birth when they go to walk among the stars. Our dead never forget this beautiful earth, for it is the mother of the red man.

We are part of the earth and it is part of us. The perfumed flowers are our sisters; the deer, the horse, the great eagle, these are our brothers.

The rocky crests, the juices in the meadows, the body heat of the pony, and man — all belong to the same family.

So, when the Great Chief in Washington sends word that he wishes to buy our land, he asks much of us. The Great Chief sends word he will reserve us a place so that we can live comfortably to ourselves.

He will be our father and we will be his children. So we will consider your offer to buy our land.

But it will not be easy. For this land is sacred to us.

This shining water that moves in the streams and rivers is not just water but the blood of our ancestors.

If we sell you land, you must remember that it is sacred, and you must teach your children that it is sacred and that each ghostly reflection in the clear water of the lakes tells of events and memories in the life of my people.

The water's murmur is the voice of my father's father.

The rivers are our brothers, they quench our thirst. The rivers carry our canoes, and feed our children. If we sell you our land, you must remember, and teach your children, that the rivers are our brothers, and yours, and you must henceforth give the rivers the kindness you would give any brother.

We know that the white man does not understand our ways. One portion of land is the same to him as the next, for he is a stranger who comes in the night and takes from the land whatever he needs.

The earth is not his brother, but his enemy, and when he has conquered it, he moves on.

He leaves his father's grave behind, and he does not care. He kidnaps the earth from his children, and he does not care.

His father's grave and his children's birthright, are forgotten. He treats his mother, the earth, and his brother, the sky, as things to be bought, plundered, sold like sheep or bright beads.

His appetite will devour the earth and leave behind only a desert.

I do not know. Our ways are different from your ways ...

This we know: the earth does not belong to man; man belongs to the earth. This we know.

All things are connected like the blood which unites one family. All things are connected.

Whatever befalls the earth befalls the sons of the earth. Man did not weave the web of life: he is merely a strand in it. Whatever he does to the web, he does to himself.

Even the white man, whose God walks and talks with him as friend to friend, cannot be exempt from the common destiny.

We may be brothers after all.

We shall see.

One thing we know, which the white man may one day discover — our God is the same God.

You may think now that you own Him as you wish to own our land; but you cannot. He is the God of man, and His compassion is equal for the red man and the white.

This earth is precious to Him, and to harm the earth is to heap contempt on its Creator.

The whites too shall pass; perhaps sooner than all other tribes. Contaminate your bed, and you will one night suffocate in your own waste.

But in your perishing you will shine brightly, fired by the strength of the God who brought you to this land and for some special purpose gave you dominion over this land and over the red man.

That destiny is a mystery to us, for we do not understand when the buffalo are all slaughtered, the wild horses are tamed, the secret corners of the forest heavy with scent of many men, and the view of the ripe hills blotted by talking wires.

Where is the thicket? Gone

Where is the eagle? Gone

The end of living and the beginning of survival.

Major Sullivan Ballou

Major Sullivan Ballou, an American Civil War soldier, wrote this famous and moving letter to his wife, Sarah, on July 14th, 1861. He was killed a week later, at the first Battle of Bull Run, as he clearly suspected would happen.

Sarah my love for you is deathless, it seems to bind me with mighty cables that nothing but Omnipotence could break; and yet my love of Country comes over me like a strong wind and bears me unresistibly on with all these chains to the battle field.

The memories of the blissful moments I have spent with you come creeping over me, and I feel most gratified to God and you that I have enjoyed them so long. And hard it is for me to give them up and burn to ashes the hopes of future years, when, God willing, we might still have lived and loved together, and seen our sons grown up to honorable manhood, around us. I have, I know, but few and small claims upon Divine Providence, but something whispers to me — perhaps it is the wafted prayer of my little Edgar, that I shall return to my loved ones unharmed. If I do not my dear Sarah, never forget how much I love you, and when my last breath escapes me on the battle field, it will whisper your name ...

But, O Sarah! if the dead can come back to this earth and flit unseen around those they loved, I shall always be near you; in the gladdest days and in the darkest nights ... *always, always*, and if there be a soft breeze upon your cheek, it shall be my breath, as the cool air fans your throbbing temple, it shall be my spirit passing by. Sarah do not mourn me dead; think I am gone and wait for thee, for we shall meet again.

...

Abraham Lincoln

Abraham Lincoln (1809—65) was the sixteenth President of the United States, holding office during the Civil War (1861—65). He wrote to Mrs Lydia Bixby, whose five sons had all died fighting to preserve the Union. Lincoln himself was assassinated the following year. The letter is dated November 21st, 1864.

To MRS BIXBY, Boston, Mass.

Dear Madam,

I have been shown in the files of the War Department a statement of the Adjutant-General of Massachusetts that you are the mother of five sons who have died gloriously on the field of battle. I feel how weak and fruitless must be any word of mine which should attempt to beguile you from the grief of a loss so overwhelming. But I cannot refrain from tendering you the consolation that may be found in the thanks of the republic they died to save. I pray that our Heavenly Father may assuage the anguish of your bereavement, and leave you only the cherished memory of the loved and lost, and the solemn pride that must be yours to have laid so costly a sacrifice upon the altar of freedom.

Yours very sincerely and respectfully,
A. Lincoln

...

Karl Marx

Karl Marx (1818—83), German philosopher, economist and revolutionary social theorist, lived for much of his life in England. He produced his three-volume work *Das Kapital* over a period of many years. He wrote about this work, which laid out the fundamentals of Marxism, to Karl Klings, a leading member of the General German Workers Association. This letter is dated October 4th, 1864.

I have been ill for the whole of this last year (carbuncles and furuncles) — Without that, my work, *Capital*, on political economy would have been published already. Now I hope to finish it in a couple of months and to deal a theoretical blow to the bourgeoisie from which they will never recover.

Farewell and rely on it that the working class will always find a loyal champion in me.

...

Susan B. Anthony

Susan B. Anthony (1820—1906), American women's rights activist, came from a Quaker family in which the eight children were encouraged to study and better themselves. Anthony's interest in the women's movement was fired by her father's enthusiastic reports of Elizabeth Cady Stanton's resolution demanding women's suffrage. Anthony never married and dedicated most of her life to the struggle for women's rights, helping to found the International Council of Women, and editing the newspaper the *Revolution*. This letter to Stanton was written on November 5th, 1872, the day she appeared at the polling station in Rochester, New York, with 50 of her friends, and cast the first ever vote by a woman in American history. Her action was followed by a prosecution, but the resultant publicity helped to gain support for women's suffrage.

Well, I have gone and done it!! — positively voted the Republican ticket — Strait — this A.M. at 7 o'clock — & swore my vote in at that ... All my three sisters voted — Rhoda de Garmo too — Amy Post was rejected & she will immediately bring action against the registrars ... Not a jeer not a word — not a look —

disrespectful has met a single woman ... I hope the morning's telegrams will tell of many women all over the country trying to vote ... I hope you voted too.

...

General Charles George Gordon

In 1884, the Sudanese sheik Muhammad Ahmed, known as the Mahdi, led a religious revolt against Egypt, which was at that time under British dominion. General Charles George Gordon (1833—85) was sent to Khartoum, the capital of Sudan, to rescue the beseiged British army, but himself came under seige. The British government refused to send reinforcements until it was too late and he died two days before help arrived on January 26th, 1885. In this letter, dated December 14th, 1884, he wrote to Major Watson, who was stationed in Cairo, of the impending fall of Khartoum.

My dear Watson,
I think the game is up and send Mrs Watson, you & Graham my adieux. We may expect a catastrophe in the town, on or after 10 days time. This would not have happened (if it does happen) if our people had taken better precautions as to informing us, of their movements, but this is 'spilt milk'. Good bye, Mind & let my brother (68 Elm Park Road, Chelsea) know what I owe you.
Yours sincerely
C. G. Gordon

...

Émile Zola

Émile Zola (1840—1902), French novelist, was the author of 'J'accuse', the trenchant letter to President François Félix Faure of France, printed in the newspaper L'Aurore, protesting at the treatment of Alfred Dreyfus, a Jewish army officer who had been falsely convicted of treason in 1894. When the letter was published in January 1898, Zola was prosecuted and fled to England. The Dreyfus case was eventually re-opened but it was not until 1906 that the verdict was finally reversed, and Dreyfus was granted a pardon.

Mr President,
Permit me, I beg you, in return for the gracious favours you once accorded me, to be concerned with regard to your just glory and to tell you that your record, so fair and fortunate thus far, is now threatened with the most shameful, the most ineffaceable blot.
You escaped safe and sane from the basest calumnies; you conquered all hearts. You seem radiant in the glory of a patriotic celebration ... and are preparing to preside over the solemn triumph of our Universal Exposition, which is to crown our great century of work, truth and liberty. But what a clod of mud is flung

upon your name — I was about to say your reign — through this abominable Dreyfus affair. A court martial has but recently, by order, dared to acquit one Esterhazy — a supreme slap at all truth, all justice! And it is done; France has this brand upon her visage; history will relate that it was during your administration that such a social crime could be committed.

Since they have dared, I too shall dare. I shall tell the truth because I pledge myself to tell it if justice, regularly empowered, did not do so, fully, unmitigatedly. My duty is to speak; I have no wish to be an accomplice. My nights would be haunted by the spectre of the innocent being, expiating under the most frightful torture, a crime he never committed.

And it is to you, Mr. President, that I shall out this truth, with all the force of my revolt as an honest man. To your honour, I am convinced that you are ignorant of the crime. And to whom, then, shall I denounce the malignant rabble of true culprits, if not to you, the highest magistrate in the country? ...

I accuse Colonel du Paty de Clam of having been the diabolical agent of the judicial error, unconsciously, I prefer to believe, and of having continued to defend his deadly work during the past three years through the most absurd and revolting machinations.

I accuse General Mercier of having made himself an accomplice in one of the greatest crimes of history, probably through weakmindedness.

I accuse General Billot of having had in his hands the decisive proofs of the innocence of Dreyfus and of having concealed them, and of having rendered himself guilty of the crime of lèse humanity and lèse justice, out of political motives and to save the face of the General Staff.

I accuse General Boisdeffre and General Gonse of being accomplices in the same crime, the former no doubt through religious prejudice, the later out of *esprit de corp*s.

I accuse General de Pellieux and Major Ravary of having made a scoundrelly inquest, I mean an inquest of the most monstrous partiality, the complete report of which composes for us an imperishable monument of naïve effrontery.

I accuse the three handwriting experts, MM. Belhomme, Varinard and Couard, of having made lying and fraudulent reports, unless a medical examination will certify them to be deficient of sight and judgement.

I accuse the War Office of having led a vile campaign in the press, particularly in *l'Eclair* and *l'Echo de Paris*, in order to misdirect public opinion and cover up its sins.

I accuse, lastly, the first court martial of having violated all human right in condemning a prisoner on testimony kept secret from him, and I accuse the second court martial of having covered up this illegality by order, committing in turn the judicial crime of acquitting a guilty man with full knowledge of his guilt.

In making these accusations I am aware that I render myself liable to articles 30 and 31 of Libel Laws of July 29th, 1881, which punish acts of defamation. I expose myself voluntarily.

As to the men I accuse, I do not know them, I have never seen them, I feel neither resentment nor hatred against them. For me they are only entities, emblems of social malfeasance. The action I take here is simply a revolutionary step designed to hasten the explosion of truth and justice.

I have one passion only, for light, in the name of humanity which has borne so much and has a right to happiness. My burning protest is only the cry of my soul. Let them dare, then, to carry me to the court of appeals, and let there be an inquest in the full light of the day!

I am waiting.

Mr. President, I beg you to accept the assurances of my deepest respect.

Émile Zola

...

Captain Robert Falcon Scott

Captain Robert Falcon Scott (1868—1912), the English explorer, led two expeditions to the Antarctic to try to reach the South Pole. On the second attempt he reached the Pole, only to find that his great rival, the Norwegian Roald Amundsen, had beaten him in the race. Scott and his companions perished on the return journey. This letter to the mother of Lieutenant H. R. Bowers, one of the men who died with him, was written in March 1912 and found with their bodies.

My dear Mrs. Bowers,

I am afraid that this will reach you after one of the heaviest blows of your life.

I write when we are very near the end of our journey, and I am finishing it in company with two gallant, noble gentlemen. One of these is your son. He had come to be one of my closest and soundest friends, and I appreciate his wonderful upright nature, his ability and energy. As the troubles have thickened his dauntless spirit ever shone brighter and he has remained cheerful, hopeful, and indomitable to the end.

The ways of Providence are inscrutable, but there must be some reason why such a young, vigorous and promising life is taken.

My whole heart goes out in pity for you.

Yours,

R. Scott

To the end he has talked of you and his sisters. One sees what a happy home he must have had and perhaps it is well to look back on nothing but happiness.

He remains unselfish, self-reliant and splendidly hopeful to the end, believing in God's mercy to you.

...

Wilfred Owen

Wilfred Owen (1893—1918), English poet of the First World War, was killed in action a week before the Armistice, on November 4th, 1918. This letter was written to his mother, Susan, on October 4th, 1918.

Strictly private
In the field

My darling Mother,

As you must have known both by my silence and from the newspapers which mention this Division — and perhaps by other means & senses — I have been in action for some days.

I can find no word to qualify my experiences except the word SHEER. (Curiously enough I find the papers talk about sheer fighting!) It passed the limits of my Abhorrence. I lost all my earthly faculties, and fought like an angel.

If I started into detail of our engagement I should disturb the censor and my own Rest.

You will guess what has happened when I say I am now Commanding the Company, and in the line had a boy lance-corporal as my Sergeant-Major.

With this corporal who stuck to me and shadowed me like your prayers I captured a German Machine Gun and scores of prisoners.

I'll tell you exactly how another time. I only shot one man with my revolver (at about 30 yards!); The rest I took with a smile. The same thing happened with other parties all along the line we entered.

I have been recommended for the Military Cross; and have recommended every single N.C.O. who was with me!

My nerves are in perfect order.

I came out in order to help these boys — directly by leading them as well as an officer can; indirectly, by watching their sufferings that I may speak of them as well as a pleader can. I have done the first.

Of whose blood lies yet crimson on my shoulder where his head was — and where so lately yours was — I must not now write.

It is all over for a long time. We are marching steadily back.

Moreover
The War is nearing an end.
Still,
     Wilfred and more than Wilfred

...

Edward, Prince of Wales

In January 1936, on the death of George V, the Prince of Wales became King Edward VIII. In December of the same year he abdicated, without having been crowned. The Abdication Crisis, which rocked the British monarchy, was precipitated by his determination to marry the twice-divorced American, Wallis Warfield Simpson. This was the letter he wrote to parliament on December 10th, 1936, announcing his decision to abdicate.

After long and anxious consideration I have determined to renounce the throne to which I succeeded on the death of my father and I am now communicating this my final and irrevocable decision. Realizing as I do the gravity of this step, I can only hope that I shall have the understanding of my people in the decision I have taken, and the reasons which have led me to take it.

I will not enter now into my private feelings, but I would beg that it should be remembered that the burden which constantly rests upon the shoulders of a sovereign is so heavy that it can only be borne in circumstances different from those in which I find myself.

I conceive that I am not overlooking the duty that rests on me to place in the forefront the public interest when I declare that I am conscious that I can no longer discharge this heavy task with the efficiency or with the satisfaction to myself. I have accordingly this morning executed an instrument of abdication in the terms following:

I, Edward VIII, of Great Britain, Ireland and the British Dominions beyond the seas, King, Emperor of India, do hereby declare my irrevocable determination to renounce the throne for myself and for my descendants and my desire that effect should be given to this instrument of abdication immediately.

In token whereof I have here unto set my hand this 10th day of December, 1936, in the presence of the witnesses whose signatures are subscribed.

    Signed Edward R. I.

...

Canute Frankson

In 1936, when Spain erupted into Civil War, men and women from many countries rallied to the struggle against Fascism and joined the International Brigades. In America almost 3000 volunteers joined the Abraham Lincoln Brigade. Included in these were 80 African Americans, among them Canute Frankson, who wrote to a friend on July 6th, 1937, to give his reasons for joining the cause.

My Dear Friend:

I'm sure that by this time you are still waiting for a detailed explanation of what has this international struggle to do with my being here. Since this is a war between whites who for centuries have held us in slavery, and have heaped every kind of insult and abuse upon us, segregated and jim-crowed us; why I, a Negro, who have fought through these years for the rights of my people, am here in Spain today?

Because we are no longer an isolated minority group fighting hopelessly against an immense giant. Because, my dear, we have joined with, and become an active part of, a great progressive force, on whose shoulders rests the responsibility of saving human civilization from the planned destruction of a small group of degenerates gone mad in their lust for power. Because if we crush Fascism here, we'll save our people in America, and in other parts of the world, from the vicious persecution, wholesale imprisonment, and slaughter which the Jewish people suffered and are suffering under Hitler's Fascist heels ...

... We will crush them. We will build us a new society — a society of peace and plenty. There will be no color line, no jim-crow trains, no lynching. That is why, my dear, I'm here in Spain ...

On the battlefields of Spain we fight for the preservation of democracy. Here, we're laying the foundation for world peace, and for the liberation of my people, and of the human race. Here, where we're engaged in one of the most bitter struggles of human history, there is no color line, no discrimination, no race hatred. There's only one hate, and that is the hate for fascism ...

Salud.
Canute

...

Rt. Hon. Neville Chamberlain

As the Second World War loomed, the Rt. Hon. Neville Chamberlain (1869—1940), Prime Minister of Britain, wrote to the German Chancellor, Adolf Hitler, in an attempt to continue negotiations and avert the outbreak of hostilities. This letter is dated August 22nd, 1939.

Your Excellency,

Your Excellency will have already heard of certain measures taken by His Majesty's Government, and announced in the Press and on the wireless this evening.

These steps have, in the opinion of His Majesty's Government, been rendered necessary by the military movements which have been reported from Germany, and by the fact that apparently the announcement of a German-Soviet Agreement is taken in some quarters in Berlin to indicate that intervention by Great Britain on behalf of Poland is no longer a contingency that need be reckoned with. No greater mistake could be made. Whatever may prove to be the nature of the German-Soviet Agreement, it cannot alter Great Britain's obligation to Poland which His Majesty's Government have stated in public repeatedly and plainly, and which they are determined to fulfil.

It has been alleged that, if His Majesty's Government had made their position more clear in 1914, the great catastrophe would have been avoided. Whether or not there is any force in that allegation, His Majesty's Government are resolved that on this occasion there shall be no such tragic misunderstanding.

If the case should arise, they are resolved, and prepared, to employ without delay all the forces at their command, and it is impossible to foresee the end of hostilities once engaged. It would be a dangerous illusion to think that, if war once starts, it will come to an early end even if a success on any one of the several fronts on which it will be engaged should have been secured.

Having thus made our position perfectly clear, I wish to repeat to you my conviction that war between our two peoples would be the greatest calamity that could occur. I am certain that it is desired neither by our people, nor by yours, and I cannot see that there is anything in the questions arising between Germany and Poland which could not and should not be solved without the use of force, if only a situation of confidence could be restored to enable discussions to be carried on in an atmosphere different from that which prevails today ...

In view of the grave consequences to humanity, which may follow from the action of their rulers, I trust that Your Excellency will weigh with the utmost deliberation the considerations which I

have put before you.
    Your sincerely
        Neville Chamberlain

...

Stanley Lupino

In October 1940, Stanley Lupino (1893—1942) wrote this letter to his wife, Ida
Lupino, an actress who was living with their daughter in America. Stanley Lupino
had remained in London and worked as an A.R.P. (Air Raid Precautions) warden.
The letter was written during the intense bombing of July to October 1940, which
came to be known as the Battle of Britain. The population sought sanctuary in the
bomb shelters and it was the A.R.P. warden's duty to patrol the streets, sending
people to shelter and warning them of unexploded bombs.

The Battle of London is on. They are trying all the devilment
that hell can supply them with, but it will not avail them one iota
towards victory. There is hardly a district that is unfortified that
they have not bombed. But they cannot beat the Cockney spirit. It
is so wonderful that if I could try and even tell you, you would
scarcely believe it. Homeless people sitting on their few belongings
in the road, singing 'There'll Always Be an England', 'Daisy, Daisy'
and hymns.

Us A.R.P. wardens have been at work from sunrise to sunrise. I
have had 2 hours' sleep in one week (in bed). The intensified gun
barrage we are putting up is so terrific all the birds in the trees are
fallen dead in thousands. It is unceasing, the sky aflame with shells
bursting like thousands of red hot stars and shrapnel falling like
rain. We do all our rounds in complete darkness, and in dashes run,
fall flat, wait, run, and so on.

My shelter is crammed. They sleep in it all night. Women,
babies, and three guards who take it in turns to doze, and take duty.
I've had to improvise a small block house at the top in the coal
cellar, shoved up, to keep top duty. This is done in case the shelter
is blown in, I can get the squad to dig them out. If I'm blown in the
guards below can dig me out. Also against spies, enemy agents, and
signallers.

Likewise we have to dash to put out incendiaries, and listen for
the dull thud denoting time bombs dropped. This is the most
hazardous job, as it means searching in darkness, with only a tiny
light, for a hole. And it may go off at any time. It's a very windy job.
Two nights ago myself and one other warden were searching for 6
hours with guns and bombs going at every minute. Thank God it was
not there. It was a huge piece of shrapnel that had caused the alarm.

They don't laugh at wardens any more. They bless us and look upon us as their greatest friends in need. Children run to us when they see the familiar black tin hat with the 'W' on it in white. Conductors won't take fares from us and shops hardly want to take payment when we walk in. We are policemen, nurses, fire-fighters, watchers for danger, aids in sickness, and give comfort and confidence to all and sundry.

During the night I visit the sleeping people in shelters. I never speak, only stand and inspect them, but they all say they feel my presence even in the darkness. And it gives them confidence. They know the familiar sound of my walk and the soft tread of my heavy gum boots. I never wake them, just stand in the dim light of a night light. If one wants to talk they whisper. One girl, a typist in the City, was awake in the shelter for 60 with 140 in it, huddled in heaps on the floor. She looked up and whispered, 'Hold my hand, sir, just for a minute.' I said, 'Of course.' After a while she pressed it to her face, and said, 'I feel better now. I haven't seen my man for 3 months and I'm going to have a baby. I just wanted to feel a man's hand against my face.'

This is only a few of the things that happen, choky, heart hurting things that make you have to brace up and bite your lip. It's not the bombs, or the guns, that upset you, it's the lovableness of the people. Their hearts and souls laid bare — and when laid bare, so sweet to see. Neighbours who have never exchanged a word, huddled together for warmth and pity. I saw a pale-faced boy of 18 with an old lady's head pillowed in his lap. He was stroking her hair. 'Your Mum?' I said. 'No, sir,' he replied. 'I don't know her.'

Six o'clock! The all clear heard in its welcome wail. Tired pale faces come out of holes in the ground. I make tea, to bed two hours.

The warning again. On duty. I shall not wake them. I stand seeing a terrific air battle. Gosh! It's a 4-engined Dornier. There they go. There's the A.A. letting loose. My God, they've got him. He's alight. He's falling, 7 tons of metal falling like a snow leaf. I pray it does not hit a house. There comes the crew. One of them with no parachute. German bones will smash a hole in English soil. Hitler, you're losing, you're losing. You tried to bring terror to us; it's coming to you. They tried to bomb our King and Queen who have never harmed a soul. Boy, what the R.A.F. said!

Desperate men will resort to anything. They are desperate and soon will be in terror. I want them in terror, long years of it. And it's coming. We're coming — so is the U.S.A., Australia, Canada, New Zealand, India, Egypt, Turkey, Greece and the world. But it's Britain that will break their hearts, and soon. I want them broken, beaten, smashed, and the cancer burnt out of Europe for ever and ever ...

History

Shmuel Minzberg

This letter was found in the Jewish ghetto of Shavli in Lithuania and was written on the eve of the ghetto's final liquidation.

We attest that on 7 July 1944 the order for the evacuation of the ghetto of *Shavli* was issued.

We want our names to be known for the generations to come: (1) Shmuel Minzberg, son of Shimon of the city of Lodz (Poland); (2) His wife Reizele née Saks of Vaiguva; (3) Feigele Saks, the latter's sister; and (4) Friedele Niselevitch of Vaiguva, Nahum Zvi's daughter.

We do not know to what destination they are sending us. In the ghetto 2,000 Jews are waiting for the order to leave. Our fate is unknown. Our state of mind is awful.

May the Kingdom of Israel
arrive soon, in our days.
Shmuel Minzberg

...

Valeri Valkov

This letter was written by a thirteen-year-old boy, Valeri Valkov, who produced a newssheet during the siege of Sevastopol by the German army in 1942. This was the last, number eleven, written when only ten defenders remained. Valkov threw a grenade and blew up an advancing tank, but was shot.

Dear comrades,

Whoever gets out of this alive must tell all who will study at this school. No matter where you end up come and tell them what happened here in Sevastopol. I want to be a bird and fly round all Sevastopol, to every home, every school, every street ... Hitler and the other scum will never beat us ... We are the millions, watch out! From the Far East to Riga, from the Caucasus to Kiev, from Sevastopol to Tashkent ... We, like steel, are invincible!

Valeri 'the Poet' (Volk)

...

Nikita Kruschev

In October 1962, American spy planes discovered that Soviet missiles had been installed in Cuba. There followed a two-day stand-off between the Soviet Union and the United States. American President John Fitzgerald Kennedy (1917—63) considered air strikes to destroy the missile bases, then instituted a naval blockade of Cuba. In this letter, dated October 27th, 1962, Soviet leader Nikita Kruschev (1894—1971) offered to withdraw the weapons if the U.S. did not invade Cuba. For two days the world waited in fear of nuclear war.

If assurances were given that the President of the United States would not participate in an attack on Cuba and the blockade [were] lifted, then the question of the removal or the destruction of the missile sites in Cuba would then be an entirely different question ... we and you ought not to pull on the ends of the rope in which you have tied the knot of war, because the more the two of us pull, the tighter that knot will be tied ... Let us not only relax the forces pulling the end of the rope, let us take measures to untie that knot. We are ready for this.

The American President sent off his reply the same evening, promising to lift the blockade and not to invade Cuba, provided that the Russians agreed to remove their missiles from the island and not to install any more. Krushchev's answer came on the next day, October 28th.

I have received your message of 27th October ... So as to eliminate as rapidly as possible the conflict which is endangering peace, ... the Soviet Government, in addition to the earlier instructions to cease further work on the weapon-construction sites, has given a new order to dismantle those arms which you have described as offensive, to crate them, and return them to the Soviet Union ...

...

James Baldwin

Angela Davis (b. 1944), American lecturer, writer and political activist, was devoted to eradicating poverty and oppression, particularly among blacks. Actively involved in the American Communist Party, she was tried and imprisoned for complicity in the 1970 prison break by political prisoners, including George Jackson. She was ultimately acquitted of all charges, but in the meantime, her case generated worldwide attention. It inspired the black American writer James Baldwin (1924—87) to write Davis this letter and it was included in her book *If They Come In The Morning: Voices of Resistence*.

November 19th, 1970

Dear Sister;
One might have hoped that, by this hour, the very sight of chains on Black flesh, or the very sight of chains, would be so intolerable a sight for the American people, and so unbearable a memory, that they would themselves spontaneously rise up and strike off the manacles. But, no, they appear to glory in their chains. Now, more than ever, they appear to measure their safety in chains and corpses. And so, *Newsweek*, civilized defender of the indefensible, attempts to drown you in a sea of crocodile tears ('it remained to be seen what sort of personal liberation she had achieved') and puts you on its cover, chained.

History

You look exceedingly alone — as alone, say, as the Jewish housewife in the boxcar headed for Dachau, or as any one of our ancestors, chained together in the name of Jesus, headed for a Christian land.

Well. Since we live in an age in which silence is not only criminal, but suicidal, I have been making as much noise as I can, here in Europe, on radio and television — in fact, have just returned from a land, Germany, which was made notorious by a silent majority not so very long ago. I was asked to speak on the case of Miss Angela Davis, and did so. Very probably an exercise in futility, but one must let no opportunity slide ...

What has happened, it seems to me, and to put it far too simply, is that a whole new generation of people have assessed and absorbed their history, and, in that tremendous action, have freed themselves of it and will never be victims again. This may seem an odd, indefensibly impertinent and insensitive thing to say to a sister in prison, battling for her life — for all our lives. Yet, I dare to say, for I think that you will perhaps not misunderstand me, and I do not say it, after all, from the position of a spectator.

I am trying to suggest that you — for example — do not appear to be your father's daughter in the same way that I am my father's son. At bottom, my father's expectations and mine were the same; the expectation of his generation and mine were the same and neither the immense difference in our ages nor the move from the South to the North could alter these expectations or make our lives more viable. For, in fact, to use the brutal parlance of that hour, the interior language of that despair, he was just a nigger — a nigger labourer preacher, and so was I. I jumped the track but that's of no more importance here, in itself, than the fact that *some* poor Spaniards become rich bull fighters, or that *some* poor Black boys become rich — boxers, for example. That's rarely, if ever, afforded the people more than a great emotional catharsis, though I don't mean to be condescending about that, either. But when Cassius Clay became Muhammed Ali and refused to put on that uniform (and sacrificed all that money!) a very different impact was made on the people and a very different kind of instruction had begun.

The American triumph — in which the American tragedy has always been implicit — was to make Black people despise themselves. When I was little I despised myself, I did not know any better. And this meant, albeit unconsciously, or against my will, or in great pain, that I also despised my father. *And* my mother. *And* my brothers. *And* my sisters. Black people were killing each other

161

every Saturday night out on Lenox Avenue, when I was growing up; and no one explained to them, or to me, that it was *intended* that they should; that they were penned where they were, like animals, in order that they should consider themselves no better than animals. Everything supported this sense of reality, nothing denied it: and so one was ready, when it came time to go to work, to be treated as a slave. So one was ready, when human terrors came, to bow before a white God and beg Jesus for salvation — this same white God who was unable to raise a finger to do so little as to help you pay your rent, unable to be awakened in time to help you save your child! ...

But what, in America, is the will of the people? And who, for the above-named, *are* the people? ... The will of the people, in America, has always been at the mercy of an ignorance not merely phenomenal, but sacred, and sacredly cultivated: the better to be used by a carnivorous economy which democratically slaughters and victimizes whites and Blacks alike. But most white Americans do not dare admit this (though they suspect it) and this fact contains mortal danger for the Blacks and tragedy for the nation ...

Only a handful of the millions of people in this vast place are aware that the fate intended for you, Sister Angela, and for George Jackson, and for the numberless prisoners in our concentration camps — for that is what they are — is a fate which is about to engulf them, too. White lives, for the forces which rule in this country, are no more sacred than Black ones, as many and many a student is discovering, as the white American corpses in Vietnam prove. If the American people are unable to contend with their elected leaders for the redemption of their own honour and the lives of their own children, we, the Blacks, the most rejected of the Western children, can expect very little help at their hands: which, after all, is nothing new. What the Americans do not realize is that a war between brothers, in the same cities, on the same soil, is not a *racial* war but a *civil* war. But the American delusion is not only that their brothers all are white but that the whites are all their brothers.

So be it. We cannot awaken this sleeper, and God knows we have tried. We must do what we can do, and fortify and save each other — *we* are not drowning in an apathetic self-contempt, we *do* feel ourselves sufficiently worthwhile to contend even with inexorable forces in order to change our fate and the fate of our children and the condition of the world! We know that a man is not a thing and is not to be placed at the mercy of things. We know that air and water belong to all mankind and not merely to industrialists. We

162

know that a baby does not come into the world merely to be the instrument of someone else's profit. We know that democracy does not mean the coercion of all into a deadly — and, finally, wicked — mediocrity but the liberty for all to aspire to the best that is in him, or that has ever been.

We know that we, the Blacks, and not only we, the Blacks, have been, and are, the victims of a system whose only fuel is greed, whose only god is profit. We know that the fruits of this system have been ignorance, despair, and death, and we know that the system is doomed because the world can no longer afford it — if, indeed, it ever could have. And we know that, for the perpetuation of this system, we have all been mercilessly brutalized, and have been told nothing but lies, lies about ourselves and our kinsmen and our past, and about love, life, and death, so that both soul and body have been bound in hell.

The enormous revolution in Black consciousness which has occurred in your generation, my dear sister, means the beginning of the end of America. Some of us, white and Black, know how great a price has already been paid to bring into existence a new consciousness, a new people, an unprecedented nation. If we know, and do nothing, we are worse than the murderers hired in our name.

If we know, then we must fight for your life as though it were our own — which it is — and render impassable with our bodies the corridor to the gas chamber. For, if they take you in the morning, they will be coming for us that night.

Therefore: peace.

Brother James

...

Mrs Eleanor Wimbish

This letter to William R. Stocks from his mother, Mrs Eleanor Wimbish, was left under his name on the Vietnam Veterans' Memorial in Washington D.C.

Today is February 13th, 1984. I came to this black wall again to see and touch your name, and as I do I wonder if anyone ever stops to realize that next to your name, on this black wall, is your mother's heart. A heart broken 15 years ago today, when you lost your life in Vietnam.

And as I look at your name, William R. Stocks, I think of how many, many times I used to wonder how scared and homesick you must have been in that strange country called Vietnam. And if and how it might have changed you, for you were the most happy-go-lucky kid in the world, hardly ever sad or unhappy. And until the day I die, I will see you as you laughed at me, even when I was very mad at you, and the next thing I knew, we were laughing together..

But on this past New Year's Day, I had my answer. I talked by phone to a friend of yours from Michigan, who spent your last Christmas and the last four months of your life with you. Jim told me how you died, for he was there and saw the helicopter crash. He told me how you had flown your quota and had not been scheduled to fly that day. How the regular pilot was unable to fly, and had been replaced by someone with less experience. How they did not know the exact cause of the crash. How it was either hit by enemy fire, or they hit a pole or something unknown. How the blades went through the chopper and hit you. How you lived about half an hour, but were unconscious and therefore did not suffer.

He said how your jobs were like sitting ducks. They would send you men out to draw the enemy into the open and *then* they would send in the big guns and planes to take over. Meantime, death came to so many of you …

They tell me the letters I write to you and leave here at this memorial are waking others up to the fact that there is still much pain left, after all these years, from the Vietnam War.

But this I know. I would rather to have had you for 21 years, and all the pain that goes with losing you, than never to have had you at all.

    Mom

Science
& Human
Endeavour

In a Man's Letters, you know, madam
his soul lies naked. His letters are only
the mirror of his heart ... is not my soul laid
open before you in these veracious pages?

Dr Samuel Johnson (1709—84),
English writer and critic, to Mrs Thrale, October 27th, 1777.

Enea Silvio Piccolomini

Johann Gutenberg (c. 1400—68) is considered to be the inventor of printing from movable metal type. On March 12th, 1455, Enea Silvio Piccolomini, Bishop of Siena, wrote to the Spanish Cardinal, Juan de Carvajal, concerning a remarkable encounter in Frankfurt in the preceding year. The 'remarkable man' is thought to be Gutenberg, who was responsible for printing the *Mazarin* and the *Bamberg* bibles.

Everything that has been written to me about that remarkable man whom I met in Frankfurt is quite true. I did not see complete Bibles but sections in fives of various books thereof, the text of which was absolutely free from error and printed with extreme elegance and accuracy. Your Eminence would have read them with no difficulty and without the aid of spectacles. I learned from many witnesses that 158 copies have been completed, although some asserted that the total was 180. While I am not quite sure about the actual number, I do not have any doubt, if people are to be believed, about the perfection of the volumes. If I had known what you wanted, I would undoubtedly have purchased a copy for you.

Some of the sections have been sent here to the Emperor. I will try, if it can be arranged, to have a complete Bible that is for sale brought here, and I will buy it on your account. I fear, however, that this may not be feasible, both because of the distance involved and because they say there have been ready buyers for the volumes, even before they are finished.

That your Eminence was most anxious to receive reliable information about this matter, I infer from your having indicated this by sending a courier who goes faster than Pegasus! But enough of this levity.

...

Leonardo da Vinci

Leonardo da Vinci (1452—1519) was one of the greatest figures of the Italian Renaissance: a painter, sculptor, architect, musician, engineer and scientist. In 1482, he wrote to Ludovico Sforza, the Duke of Milan, laying out his qualifications for employment in his service.

Having, most illustrious Lord, seen and considered the experiments of all those who pose as masters in the art of inventing instruments of war, and finding that their inventions differ in no way from those in common use, I am emboldened, without prejudice to anyone, to solicit an appointment of acquainting your Excellency with certain of my Secrets.

1. I can construct bridges which are very light and strong and very portable, with which to pursue and defeat the enemy; and others more solid, which resist fire or assault, yet are easily removed and placed in position; and I can also burn and destroy those of the enemy.

2. In case of a seige I can cut off water from the trenches and make pontoons and scaling ladders and other similar contrivances.

3. If by reason of the elevation or the strength of its position a place cannot be bombarded, I can demolish every fortress if its foundations have not been set on stone.

4. I can also make a kind of cannon which is light and easy of transport, with which to hurl small stones like hail, and of which the smoke causes great terror to the enemy, so that they suffer heavy loss and confusion.

5. I can noiselessly construct to any prescribed point subterranean passages either straight or winding, passing if necessary underneath trenches or a river.

6. I can make armoured wagons carrying artillery, which shall break through the most serried ranks of the enemy, and so open a safe passage for his infantry,

7. If occasion should arise, I can construct cannon and mortars and light ordnance in shape both ornamental and useful and different from those in common use.

8. When it is impossible to use cannon I can supply in their stead catapults, mangonels, *trabocchi*, and other instruments of admirable efficiency not in general use — In short, as the occasion requires I can supply infinite means of attack and defence.

9. And if the fight should take place upon the sea I can construct many engines most suitable either for attack or defence and ships which can resist the fire of the heaviest cannon, and powders or weapons.

10. In time of peace, I believe that I can give you as complete satisfaction as anyone else in the construction of buildings both public and private, and in conducting water from one place to another.

I can further execute sculpture in marble, bronze or clay, also in painting I can do as much as anyone else, whoever he may be.

Moreover, I would undertake the commission of the bronze horse, which shall endure with immortal glory and eternal honour the auspicious memory of your father and of the illustrious house of Sforza —

And if any of the aforesaid things should seem to anyone impossible or impracticable, I offer myself as ready to make trial of them in your park or in whatever place shall please your Excellency, to whom I commend myself with all possible humility.

...

Galileo Galilei

Galileo Galilei (1564—1642) was an Italian mathematician, astronomer and physicist. He was the first to study the skies through a telescope and to deduce that the earth was not the centre of the universe, but revolved around the sun. He was tried by the Inquisition for his subversive discoveries. In this letter to Belisario Vinta, dated January 30th, 1610, he announced his discovery of four new planets.

I am at present staying at Venice for the purpose of getting printed some observations which I have been making on the celestial bodies by means of a telescope which I have, and being infinitely amazed thereat, so do I give infinite thanks to God, who has been pleased to make me the first observer of marvellous things, unrevealed to bygone ages. I had already ascertained that the moon was a body most similar to the earth, and had shown our Most Serene master as much, but imperfectly, not having such an excellent telescope which I now possess, which, besides showing me the moon, has revealed to me a multitude of fixed stars never yet seen; being more than ten times the number of those that can be seen with the unassisted eye. Moreover, I have ascertained what has always been a matter of controversy among philosophers; namely, the nature of the Milky Way.

But the greatest marvel of all is the discovery of four new planets: I have observed their proper motions in relation to themselves and to each other, and wherein they differ from all the other motions of the other stars. And these new planets move round another very great star, in the same way as Venus and Mercury, and peradventure the other known planets, move around the Sun. As soon as my tract is printed, which, as an advertisement, I intend sending to all philosophers and mathematicians, I shall send a copy to the Most Serene Grand Duke, together with an excellent telescope, which will enable him to judge for himself of the truth of these novelties.

Edmund Halley

Edmund Halley (1656—1742), English astronomer, sent this letter to Isaac Newton (1642—1727), the great English physicist and mathematician who discovered the law of gravity and created calculus. It was written on May 22nd, 1686, on the presentation of *Principia Mathematica* to the Royal Society.

Sir

Your Incomparable treatise entitled *Philosophiae Naturalis Principia Mathematica*, was by Dr Vincent presented to the R. Society on the 28th past, and they were so very sensible of the Great Honour you do them by your Dedication, that they immediately ordered you their most hearty thanks, and that a Council should be summoned to consider about the printing thereof; but by reason of the Presidents attendance upon the King, and the absence of our Vice-Presidents, whom the good weather had drawn out of Town, there has not since been any Authentic Council to resolve what to do in the matter; so that on Wednesday last the Society in their meeting, judging that so excellent a work ought not to have its publication any longer delayed, resolved to print it at their own charge, in a large Quarto, of a fair letter; and that this their resolution should be signified to you and your opinion therein be desired, that so it might be gone about with all speed. I am entrusted to look after the printing it, and will take care that it shall be performed as well as possible, only I would first have your directions in what you shall think necessary for the embellishing therof, and particularly whether you think it not better, that the Schemes should be enlarged, which is the opinion of some here; but what you signify as your desire shall be punctually observed ...

...

Lady Mary Wortley Montagu

Lady Mary Wortley Montagu (1689—1762) was a great figure of the eighteenth century and prolific letter writer, traveller and feminist. She wrote this letter to her friend, Sarah Chiswell, on April 1st, 1717, on the subject of inoculation against smallpox, which was common in Turkey. On her return to England she campaigned for the introduction of the inoculation.

Apropos of distempers, I am going to tell you a thing that I am so sure will make you wish yourself here. The smallpox, so fatal and so general amongst us, is here entirely harmless by the invention of engrafting (which is the term they give it). There is a set of old women who make it their business to perform the operation. Every autumn, in the month of September, when the great heat is abated, people send to one another to know if any of their family has a mind to have the smallpox. They make parties for this purpose, and when they are met (commonly fifteen or sixteen together) the old woman comes with a nutshell full of the matter of the best sort of smallpox and asks what veins you please to have opened. She immediately rips open that you offer to her with a large needle (which gives you no more pain than a common scratch) and puts into the vein as much venom as can lie upon the head of her needle, and after binds up the little wound with a hollow bit of shell, and in this manner opens four or five veins. The Grecians have commonly the superstition of opening one in the middle of the forehead, in each arm, and on the breast to mark the sign of the cross, but this has a very ill effect, all these wounds leaving little scars, and is not done by those that are not superstitious, who choose to have them in the legs or that part of the arm that is concealed. The children or young patients play together all the rest of the day and are in perfect health till the eighth. Then the fever begins to seize 'em and they keep their beds two days, very seldom three. They have very rarely above twenty or thirty in their faces, which never mark, and in eight days' time they are as well as before their illness. Where they are wounded there remains running sores during the distemper, which I don't doubt is a great relief to it. Every year thousands undergo this operation, and the French ambassador says pleasantly that they take smallpox here by way of diversion as they take the waters in other countries. There is no example of anyone that has died in it, and you may believe I am very well satisfied of the safety of the experiment since I intend to try it on my dear little son. I am a patriot enough to take pains to bring this useful invention into fashion in England, and I should not fail to write to some of our doctors very particular about it if I knew any one of 'em that I thought had virtue enough to destroy such a considerable branch of their revenue for the good of mankind, but that distemper is too beneficial to them not to expose to all their resentment the hardy wight that should undertake to put an end to it. Perhaps if I live to return I may, however, have courage to war with 'em. Upon this occasion, admire the heroism in the heart of your friend, etc.

...

Benjamin Franklin

Benjamin Franklin (1706—90), American author, scientist and statesman, wrote this letter from France to Sir Joseph Banks, President of the Royal Society, on July 27th, 1783. The 'vast Globe' referred to in the postcript is the first hot-air balloon, successfully launched by the Montgolfier brothers in France in June 1783.

... I join with you most cordially in rejoicing at the return of Peace.

I hope it will be lasting, and that mankind will at length, as they call themselves reasonable creatures, have reason and sense enough to settle their differences without cutting throats. For in my opinion *there never was a good War, or a bad Peace*.

What vast additions to the conveniences and comforts of living might mankind have acquired, if the money spent in wars had been employ'd in Works of public utility; what an extension of agriculture even to the tops of our Mountains; what Rivers rendered navigable, or joined by canals; what Bridges, Acqueducts, new Roads, and other public Works, Edifices, and Improvements, rendering England a compleat Paradise, might not have been obtain'd by spending those millions in doing good, which in the last War have been spent in doing mischief; in bringing misery into thousands of families, and destroying the lives of so many thousands of working people who might have perform'd the useful labour.

I am pleas'd with the late astronomical discoveries made by our Society. Furnish'd as all Europe now is with Academies of Science, with nice instruments and the spirit of Experiment, the progress of human knowledge will be rapid, and discoveries made of which we have at present no conception. I begin to be almost sorry I was born so soon, since I cannot have the happiness of knowing what will be known a hundred years hence.

I wish continued success to the labours of the Royal Society, and that you may long adorn their chair, being with the highest esteem,
Dear Sir,
your most obedient
and most humble servant,
B. Franklin.

Dr. Blagden will acquaint you with the experiment of a vast Globe sent up into the air, much talk'd of here at present, and which if prosecuted may furnish means of new knowledge.

...

Michael Faraday

Michael Faraday (1791—1867), English physicist and mathematician, was the first man to discover that an electric current could be produced from a magnetic field, and went on to invent the electric motor. His future wife, Sarah Barnard, was the recipient of this letter written in December 1820.

My dear Sarah — It is astonishing how much the state of the body influences the powers of the mind. I have been thinking all the morning of the very delightful and interesting letter I would send you this evening, and now I am so tired, and yet have so much to do, that my thoughts are quite giddy, and run round your image without any power of themselves to stop and admire it. I want to say a thousand kind and, believe me, heartfelt things to you, but am not master of words fit for the purpose; and still, as I ponder and think on you, chlorides, trials, oil, Davy, steel, miscellanea, mercury, and fifty other professional fancies swim before and drive me further and further into the quandary of stupidness.

From your affectionate
Michael

...

George Stephenson

George Stephenson (1781—1848), English engineer, built the first steam locomotive for passenger transport. He was also chief engineer of the Stockton and Darlington Railway, the world's first public railway. This letter, dated June 28th, 1821, was sent to Robert Stevenson, lighthouse engineer.

Sir, — With this you will receive three copies of a specification of a patent malleable iron rail invented by John Birkinshaw of Bedlington, near Morpeth ...

Those rails are so much liked in this neighbourhood, that I think in a short time they will do away with the cast iron railways.

They make a fine line for our engines, as there are so few joints compared with the other.

I have lately started on a new locomotive engine, with some improvements on the others which you saw. It has far surpassed my expectations. I am confident a railway on which my engines can work is far superior to a canal. On a long and favourable railway I would stent my engines to travel 60 miles per day with from 40 to 60 tons of goods.

They would work nearly fourfold cheaper than horses where coals are not very costly.

I merely make these observations, as I know you have been at more trouble than any man I know of in searching into the utility of railways ...

...

Florence Nightingale

Florence Nightingale (1820—1910), English nurse and hospital reformer, was the founder of the nursing profession. She took a team of nurses to the Crimean War (1853—6) and dramatically reduced the death rate with her improvements in hygiene. She wrote this letter to her friend, the surgeon William Bowman, on December 14th, 1854.

... On Thursday last we had 1715 sick and wounded in this Hospital (among whom 120 cholera patients) and 650 severely wounded in the other Building called the General Hospital, of which we also have charge, when a message came to me to prepare for 510 wounded on our side of the Hospital who were arriving from the dreadful affair of the 5th November from Balaklava, in which battle were 1763 wounded and 442 killed, besides 96 officers wounded and 38 killed. I always expected to end my days as Hospital Matron, but I never expected to be Barrack Mistress. We had but half an hour's notice before they began landing the wounded. Between one and nine o'clock we had the mattresses stuffed, sewn up, laid down — alas! Only matting upon the floor — the men washed and put to bed, and all their wounds dressed. I wish I had time. I would write you a letter dear to a surgeon's heart. I am as good as a *Medical Times*! But oh! You Gentlemen of England who sit at Home in all the well-earned satisfaction of your successful cases, can have little Idea from reading the newspapers of Horror and Misery (in a Military Hospital) of operating upon these dying, exhausted men. A London Hospital is a Garden of Flowers to it.

...

Alexander Graham Bell

Alexander Graham Bell (1847—1922), inventor, was born in Edinburgh. He emigrated to Canada in 1870 and then to the United States, where he invented the telephone in 1876. This comment was made in 1878.

I believe, in the future, wires will unite the head offices of the Telephone Company in different cities, and a man in one part of the country may communicate by word of mouth with another in a distant place.

...

Louis Pasteur

Louis Pasteur (1822—95), French chemist and microbiologist, was one of the most influential figures of nineteenth-century science. He pioneered vaccinations for rabies, anthrax and chicken cholera, and proved that disease caused by micro-organisms could be prevented by the process of heating that came to be called pasteurization. This letter, dated June 2nd, 1881, was written in great excitement to his family, on the first successful attempts at vaccination against anthrax.

It is only Thursday, and I am already writing to you; it is because a great result is now acquired. A wire from Melun has just announced it. On Tuesday last, 31st May, we inoculated all the sheep, vaccinated and non-vaccinated with very virulent splenic fever. It is not forty-eight hours ago. Well, the telegram tells me that, when we arrive at two o'clock this afternoon, all the non-vaccinated subjects will be dead; eighteen were already dead this morning, and the others dying. As to the vaccinated ones, they are all well; the telegram ends by the words 'stunning success', it is from the veterinary surgeon, M. Rossignol.

It is too early yet for a final judgement; the vaccinated sheep might yet fall ill. But when I write to you on Sunday, if all goes well, it may be taken for granted that they will henceforth preserve their good health, and that the success will indeed have been startling. On Tuesday, we had a foretaste of the final results. On Saturday and Sunday, two sheep had been abstracted from the lot of twenty-five vaccinated sheep, and two from the lot of twenty-five non-vaccinated ones, and inoculated with a very virulent virus. Now, when on Tuesday all the visitors arrived, amongst whom were M. Tisserand, M. Patinot, the Prefect of Seine et Marne, M. Foucher de Careil, Senator, etc., we found the two unvaccinated sheep dead, and two others in good health. I then said to one of the veterinary surgeons who were present, 'Did I not read in a newspaper, signed by you, à propos of the virulent little organism of saliva, "There! one more microbe; when there are 100 we shall make a cross." 'It is true,' he immediately answered, honestly. 'But I am a converted and repentant sinner.' 'Well, I answered, allow me to remind you of the words of the Gospel: Joy shall be in heaven over one sinner that repenteth, more than over ninety and nine just persons which need no repentance.' ... Joy reigns in the laboratory and in the house. Rejoice, my dear children.

...

Alfred Mayer

Thomas Edison (1847—1931), American scientist and prolific inventor, was responsible for many of the most important innovations of the late nineteenth and early twentieth centuries, including the phonograph-gramophone. He was also instrumental in developing the early cinema. Alfred Mayer, Professor of Physics at the Stevens Institute, wrote this letter to Edison after witnessing a demonstration of the phonograph in January 1878.

Ever since my return home your marvellous invention has so occupied my brain that I can hardly collect my thoughts to carry on my work. The results are far reaching (in science), its *capabilities* are *immense*. I cannot express my admiration of your genius better than by frankly saying that I would rather be the discoverer of your talking machine than to have made the first best discovery of any one who has worked in Acoustics.

...

Charles Darwin

Charles Darwin (1809—82) was the great English naturalist who developed the theory of evolution after extensive journeys on his ship, the *Beagle*. He published *The Origin of Species* in 1859, arousing great and continuing controversy because it refuted the book of *Genesis*. On February 26th, 1867 he wrote to fellow naturalist A. R. Wallace about his first thoughts on another book that was to become *The Descent of Man and Selection in Relation to Sex*, published in 1871.

With respect to the beauty of male butterflies, I must as yet think that it is due to sexual selection. There is some evidence that dragon-flies are attracted by bright colours; but what leads me to the above belief, is so many male Orthoptera and Cicadas having musical instruments. This being the case, the analogy of birds makes me believe in sexual selection with respect to colour in insects. I wish I had strength and time to make some of the experiments suggested by you, but I thought butterflies would not pair in confinement. I am sure I have heard of some such difficulty. Many years ago I had a dragon-fly painted with gorgeous colours, but I never had an opportunity of fairly trying it.

The reason of my being so much interested just at present about sexual selection is, that I have almost resolved to publish a little essay on the origin of Mankind, and I still strongly think (though I failed to convince you, and this, to me, is the heaviest blow possible) that sexual selection has been the main agent in forming the races of man.

By the way, there is another subject which I shall introduce in my essay, namely, expression of countenance. Now, do you happen to know by any odd chance a very good-natured and acute observer in the Malay Archipelago, who you think would make a few easy observations for me on the expression of the Malays when excited by various emotions? For in this case I would send to such person a list of queries.

Darwin said of religion, 'Disbelief crept over me at a very slow rate but was at last complete. The rate was so slow that I felt no distress.' Darwin wrote this letter explaining his position on the existence of God to an unknown recipient on November 24th, 1880.

Down,
Beckenham,
Kent.

Railway Station
Orpington
S.E.R.

Dear Sir
I am sorry to inform you that I do not believe in the Bible as a divine revelation, & therefore not in Jesus Christ as the son of God.
yours faithfully
Ch. Darwin

...

Marie and Pierre Curie

Marie Curie (1867—1934) was born Marie Sklodovska in Poland. She married Pierre Curie (1859—1906) in 1895 and together they discovered radioactivity, for which they were awarded the Nobel prize for physics. After her husband's sudden death, she continued their work alone, pioneering the use of x-rays in medicine and becoming the first woman to teach at the Sorbonne. She was awarded a second Nobel prize for chemistry for the isolation of pure radium. In this letter, dated August 10th, 1894, Pierre Curie wrote to Marie Sklodovska in Poland, asking her to return to work with him and trying to persuade her to spend her life with him.

Nothing could have given me greater pleasure than to get news of you. The prospect of remaining two months without hearing about you had been extremely disagreeable to me: that is to say, your little note was more than welcome.

I hope you are laying up a stock of good air and that you will come back to us in October. As for me, I think I shall not go anywhere; I shall stay in the country, where I spend the whole day in front of my open window or in the garden.

We have promised each other — haven't we? — to be at least great friends. If you will only not change your mind! For there are no promises that are binding; such things cannot be ordered at will. It would be a fine thing, just the same, in which I hardly dare believe, to pass our lives near each other, hypnotized by our dreams: *your* patriotic dreams, *our* humanitarian dream, and *our* scientific dream.

Of all those dreams the last is, I believe, the only legitimate one. I mean by that that we are powerless to change the social order, and even if we were not, we should not know what to do; in taking action, no matter in what direction, we should never be sure of not doing more harm than good, by retarding some inevitable evolution. From the scientific point of view, on the contrary, we may hope to do something; the ground is solider here, and any discovery that we may make, however small, will remain acquired knowledge.

See how it works out: it is agreed that we shall be great friends, but if you leave France in a year it would be an altogether too Platonic friendship, that of two creatures who would never see each other again. Wouldn't it be better for you to stay with me? I know that this question angers you, and that you don't want to speak of it again — and then, too, I feel so thoroughly unworthy of you from every point of view.

I thought of asking your permission to meet you *by chance* in Fribourg. But you are staying there, unless I am mistaken, only one day, and on that day you will of course belong to our friends the Kovalskis.

Believe me your very devoted
Pierre Curie

...

Guglielmo Marconi

Guglielmo Marconi (1874—1937), Italian pioneer in the invention and development of wireless telegraphy, conducted many of his experiments in England. In 1895 he achieved the first wireless communication. In 1903, he transmitted these wireless messages between the American President Theodore Roosevelt and King Edward VII of Britain.

The President's message read:

His Majesty, Edward VII
London, Eng.

In taking advantage of the wonderful triumph of scientific research and ingenuity which has been achieved in perfecting a system of wireless telegraphy, I extend on behalf of the American people most cordial greetings and good wishes to you and all the people of the British Empire.

Theodore Roosevelt   Wellfleet, Mass., Jan.19, 1903.

The reply from the King came back:

> Sandringham, Jan. 19, 1903
> The President,
> White House, Washington, America

I thank you most sincerely for the kind message which I have just received from you, through Marconi's trans-Atlantic wireless telegraphy. I sincerely reciprocate in the name of the people of the British Empire the cordial greetings and friendly sentiment expressed by you on behalf of the American Nation and I heartily wish you and your country every possible prosperity.

Edward R. and I.

...

Orville Wright

This telegram was sent by Orville Wright (1871—1948) to his father, Milton Wright, on the successful completion of the first powered flight, made from Kitty Hawk Sands in North Carolina on December 17th, 1903. (The time was wrongly given by the telegrapher as 57 instead of 59 seconds and Orville's name was misspelt.)

> 176 C KA CS 33 Paid.   Via Norfolk Va
> Kitty Hawk N C Dec 17
> Bishop M Wright
> 7 Hawthorne St

Success four flights thursday morning all against twenty one mile wind started from Level with engine power alone speed through air thirty one miles longest 57 second inform Press home Christmas.

> Orevelle
> Wright   525F

...

Henri Poincaré and Marie Curie

Albert Einstein (1879—1955), German-Swiss scientist, revolutionized science with his theories of relativity and gravitation. He published *The Special Theory of Relativity* in 1905 when he was only 26 years old. Two great scientists, Henri Poincaré and Marie Curie wrote this recommendation in 1911 to enable Einstein to procure a position at the Federal Institute of Technology in Zurich.

Herr Einstein is one of the most original minds that we have ever met. In spite of his youth he already occupies a very honourable position among the foremost savants of his time. What we marvel at him, above all, is the ease with which he adjusts himself to new conceptions and draws all possible deductions from them. He does not cling to classical principles, but sees all conceivable possibilities when he is confronted with a physical problem. In his mind this becomes transformed into an anticipation of new phenomena that may some day be verified in actual experience ... The future will give more and more proofs of the merits of Herr Einstein, and the University that succeeds in attaching him to itself may be certain that it will derive honour from its connection with the young master.

　　　Henri Poincaré
　　　Marie Curie

...

Carl Jung

Sigmund Freud (1856—1939), Austrian neurologist, is considered to be the founder of psychoanalysis. On December 19th, 1912, Carl Jung (1875—1961), Swiss psychiatrist and an early collaborator of Freud's, wrote to him questioning his methods. It was a disagreement from which the relationship never recovered.

　　Dear Professor Freud,
　　May I say a few words to you in earnest? I admit the ambivalence of my feelings towards you, but am inclined to take an honest and absolutely straightforward view of the situation. If you doubt my word, so much the worse for you. I would, however, point out that your technique of treating your pupils like patients is a *blunder*. In that way you produce either slavish sons or impudent puppies ... I am objective enough to see through your little trick. You go around sniffing out all the symptomatic actions in your vicinity, thus reducing everyone to the level of sons and daughters who blushingly admit the existence of their faults. Meanwhile you remain on top as the father, sitting pretty. For sheer obsequiousness nobody dares to pluck the prophet by the beard and inquire for once what you would say to a patient with a tendency to analyse the analyst instead of himself. You would certainly ask him: '*Who's* got the neurosis?'
　　You see, my dear Professor, so long as you hand out this stuff I don't give a damn for my symptomatic actions; they shrink to nothing in comparison with the formidable beam in my brother Freud's eye. I am not in the least neurotic — touch wood! I have submitted *lege artis et tout humblement* to analysis and am much the better for it. You know, of course, how far a patient gets with self-analysis: *not* out of his neurosis — just like you. If ever you should rid yourself entirely of your complexes and stop playing the father to your sons and instead of aiming continually at their weak spots took a good look at your own for a change, then I will

mend my ways and at one stroke uproot the vice of being in two minds about you. Do you *love neurotics* enough to be always at one with yourself? But perhaps you *hate* neurotics. In that case how can you expect your efforts to treat your patients leniently and lovingly *not* to be accompanied by somewhat mixed feelings? Adler and Stekel were taken in by your little tricks and reacted with childish insolence. I shall continue to stand by you publicly while maintaining my own views, but privately shall start telling you in my letters what I really think of you. I consider this procedure only decent.

No doubt you will be outraged by this peculiar token of friendship, but it may do you good all the same.

With best regards,

Most sincerely yours, JUNG

...

Marie Stopes

Marie Stopes (1880—1958), English scientist, at first specialized in fossil plants and engineering. She turned her attention to marital problems after the breakdown of her own first marriage and began to disseminate information about birth control. Her 1916 publication, *Married Love*, provoked much controversy and was banned in the United States. She opened the first birth control clinic in London in 1921. This was one of the many letters written to her.

... I married a man in the year 1912 at the age of 18, he being 22 years older year after I found I was to become a Mother (the child was still born which Was cause throught fright 3 or 4 days before. And that nearly corst me my life) My Husband having to chrilder of his own at the time boy 3 and a girl 7, which are now 18 and 21. After that it was not till 1917 that I was in London and there waiting to go in the City Rd Hospital to be confined. (I was a lone in Lodging and had to Walk a mile in Angoing while the Air Raids was on. I just got to the Door and Callopsed, the Child beining bone almost at once. 13 months after I had a nother girl bone a hour before I could sent for help. 2 year later a boy, and 2 year later another boy, this last boy have shutter my nerves (for 2 months before he was Born I had nurses from the Guild Hall to dress my Varcass Vain. The last month I walk on Sticks and they come trice aday (the Weaight of the child cause the Vain to come to such a terrible size that the chair bottom had to be removed I had to sleep with legs up) he was born on the 6th of Oct and 24 hours after I found I had got to be stitched. When I got up I had a large lump form in the Brest. I went to the Hospital and they operated 16 stitches I had. I was there 4 weeks all my chrilen being in the

180

Wookhouse I cam out to fetch the chrilden, and 2 months after the other brest was very bad I went up at 1 oclock to have to opration 12 stiches and walk home at 5. I could not have a days rest I still had to keep on, after I had to go for the Dressings Twice a day pushing 2 kiddies in the pram till at the week end my leg gave way and I had to stay four hours and wait for a letter, to say that I could go in the Calvasing Homes. I said yes, I did not go; the worry brought on a groth in my ear, I have to have it Lance. My trouble are my own, I have no simpathy hear the last day I saw was the 15th of Dec; It was on Boxing Night I conceived I have tried many Pills but Have not seen the desired effect. Please Help me! I have Had my share (I have never taken anything before) But I am frighten to Death, With what I have gone through. My life is only a living Hell.

Note: the spellings are as in the original letter

...

Sir Frank Whittle

Sir Frank Whittle (1907—96), English aviation engineer and pilot, invented the jet engine in 1937. The first flight took place in 1941. This letter was sent by R. Dudley Williams who had been a fellow air cadet at Cranwell and had been interested in Whittle's idea for a turbo jet.

This is just a hurried note to tell you that I have just met a man who is a bit of a big noise in an engineering concern and to whom I mentioned your invention of an aeroplane, *sans* propeller as it were, and who is very interested. You told me some time ago that Armstrong's had or were taking it up and if they have broken down or you don't like them, he would, I think, like to handle it. I wonder if you would write and let me know.

...

Albert Einstein

When Adolf Hitler came to power in 1933, Albert Einstein renounced his German citizenship for the second time, and left Europe for the United States. Although a pacifist, he urged Europe to arm itself against the Nazis. On August 2nd, 1939, Einstein signed a letter drafted with Leo Szilard, to the President of the United States, Franklin Delano Roosevelt. The letter led to the establishment of an advisory committee on uranium. It was the British breakthrough towards constructing the bomb that convinced the American government to initiate a fully fledged nuclear programme (the Manhattan Project).

Sir:

Some recent work by E. Fermi and L. Szilard, which has been communicated to me in manuscript, leads me to expect that the element uranium may be turned into a new and important source of energy in the immediate future. Certain aspects of the situation seem to call for watchfulness and, if necessary, quick action on the part of the administration. I believe, therefore, that it is my duty to bring to your attention the following facts and recommendations.

In the course of the last four months it has been made probable — through the work of Joliot in France as well as Fermi and Szilard in America — that it may become possible to set up nuclear chain reactions in a large mass of uranium, by which vast amounts of power and large quantities of new radium-like elements would be generated. Now it appears almost certain that this could be achieved in the immediate future.

This new phenomenon would also lead to the construction of bombs, and it is conceivable — though much less certain — that extremely powerful bombs of a new type may thus be constructed. A single bomb of this type, carried by boat or exploded in a port, might very well destroy the whole port together with some of the surrounding territory. However, such bombs might very well prove to be too heavy for transportation by air.

The United States has only very poor ores of uranium in moderate quantities. There is some good ore in Canada and the former Czechoslovakia, while the most important source of uranium is the Belgian Congo.

In view of this situation you may think it desirable to have some permanent contact between the administration and the group of physicists working on chain reaction in America. One possible way of achieving this might be for you to entrust with this task a person who has your confidence and who could perhaps serve in a unofficial capacity. The task might comprise the following:

(a) To approach government departments, keep them informed of further developments, and put forward recommendations for government action, giving particular attention to the problem of securing a supply of uranium ore for the United States.

(b) To speed up the experimental work which is at present being carried on within the limits of the budgets of the university laboratories, by providing funds, if such funds be required, through his contacts with private persons who are willing to make contributions for this cause, and perhaps also by obtaining the cooperation of industrial laboratories which have the necessary equipment.

I understand that Germany has actually stopped the sale of uranium from the Czechoslovakian mines which she has taken over. That she should have taken such early action might perhaps be understood on the ground that the son of the German Undersecretary of State, von Weizsäcker, is attached to the Kaiser Wilhelm Institute of Berlin, where some of the American work on uranium is now being repeated.

Yours very truly,
A. Einstein

index

The names of letter writers and the page references of their contributions are in bold. In the case of married women and people with titles, the reference is to the name by which the writer is most commonly known.

Index

Index

Index

acknowledgements

Every effort has been made to trace the copyright-holders of the material included in this book. In the event of any unwilling or inadvertent use of uncleared material, or for omitting the correct notification, the editor apologizes, and would be grateful to hear from the copyright-holder, and undertakes to amend any subsequent edition accordingly. The editors gratefully acknowledge permission of the following sources to use copyrighted material in this book:

The Selected Letters of Louisa May Alcott, edited by Joel Myerson and Daniel Shealy, published by Little, Brown and Company. Letters copyright © 1987 by the Estate of Theresa W. Pratt.

Selected Letters of Vanessa Bell, edited by Regina Marler, published by Bloomsbury Publishing PLC. Copyright ©1993 by Regina Marler. Reprinted courtesy of Henrietta Garnett.

Alban Berg's Letters to His Wife, edited and translated by Bernard Grun, Faber & Faber Ltd., 1971. English translations copyright © 1971 Bernard Grun. Reprinted courtesy of Eric Glass Ltd.

The Divine Sarah — A Life of Sarah Bernhardt by Arthur Gold & Robert Fizdale, copyright © 1991 by Robert Fizdale. Reprinted by permission of Alfred A. Knopf, a division of Random House, Inc.

Letters from Colette, selected and translated by Robert Phelps. Translation copyright © 1980 by Farrar Straus & Giroux, Inc. Reprinted by permission of Farrar Straus & Giroux, LLC.

Letter by Hernando Cortés from *Letters from Mexico*, translated by Anthony Pagdon, published by Yale University Press. Copyright © 1971 Anthony Pagdon.

Madame Curie by Eve Curie, published by Heinemann in 1938. Reprinted by permission of Curtis Brown Ltd.

If They Come in the Morning by Angela Davis, published by Orbach & Chambers in association with the Angela Davis Defence Committee. Copyright © 1971 by Angela Davis.

Letters from Africa 1914—1931 by Isak Dinesen, edited for the Rungstedland Foundation by Frans Lasson, translated by Anne Born, published by the University of Chicago Press. Copyright © 1981 by the University of Chicago. Originally published in two volumes as *Breve fra Afrika 1914—24* and *Breva fra Afrika 1925—31*. Copyright © 1978 by the Rungstedlund Foundation.

Letter by Albert Einstein reprinted by permission of the Albert Einstein Archives, the Jewish National and University Library, the Hebrew University of Jerusalem, Israel.

Letter by Canute Frankson from *Madrid 37: Letters of the Abraham Lincoln Brigade from the Spanish Civil War*, edited by Nelson and Hendricks, published by Routledge. Copyright © 1996 by Routledge, Inc. Reprinted by permission of Routledge, Inc., part of the Taylor & Francis Group.

The Career and Legend of Vasco da Gama, by S. Subrahmanyam, published by Cambridge University Press. Copyright © 1997 Cambridge University Press.

Collected Correspondence & Papers of Christoph Willibald Gluck, edited by Hedwig & E. H. Mueller Von Ason, Barrie & Rockcliff, London.

Johann Gutenberg: the Man and his Invention by Albert Kapr, translated by Douglas Martin, published by Scolar Press. Copyright © 1971 Albert Kapr and Douglas Martin.

Leos Janácek's letter to Kamila Stösslová from *Intimate Letters*, edited by John Tyrrell, published by Faber & Faber Ltd. and Princeton University Press. Copyright © 1994 John Tyrrell.

"A Bundle of Letters" by R. A. Johnson from *The Acorn Book of Contemporary Haiku*, edited by Lucien Stryk, published by Acorn Book Company. Copyright this poem © 2000 R. A. Johnson

Freud-Jung Letters, edited by William McGuire, published by Taylor & Francis Books Ltd. Copyright © 1974 by Sigmund Freud Copyrights Ltd. & Erbengemeinschaft Prof. Dr. C. G. Jung.

Letters to Felice by Franz Kafka, edited by Erich Heller & Jürgen Born, translated by James Stern and Elisabeth Duckworth, translation copyright © 1973 by Schocken Books, a division of Random House, Inc. Used by permission of Schocken Books, a division of Random House, Inc.

Hope Abandoned by Nadezda Mandelstam, translated by Max Hayward, published by Atheneum Publishers, New York and Harvill, London. English translation Copyright © 1972 Atheneum Publishers, New York and Harvill, London. First published in Great Britain by the Harvill Press in 1974.

191

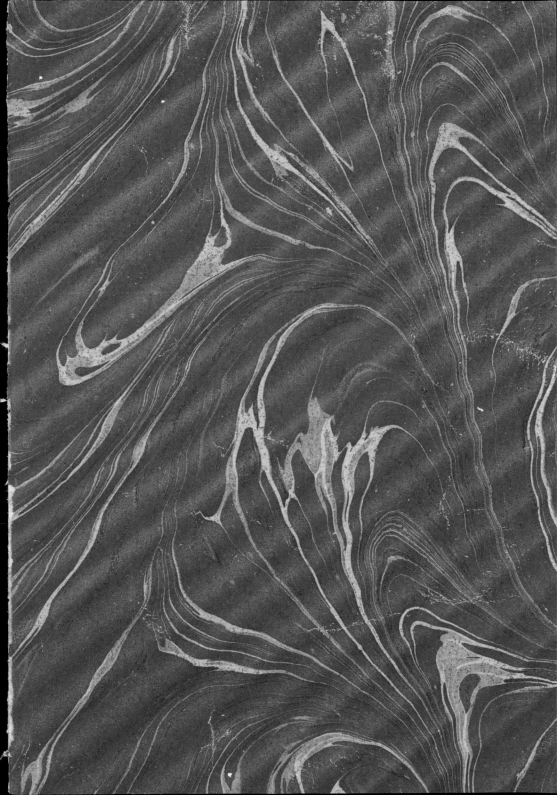

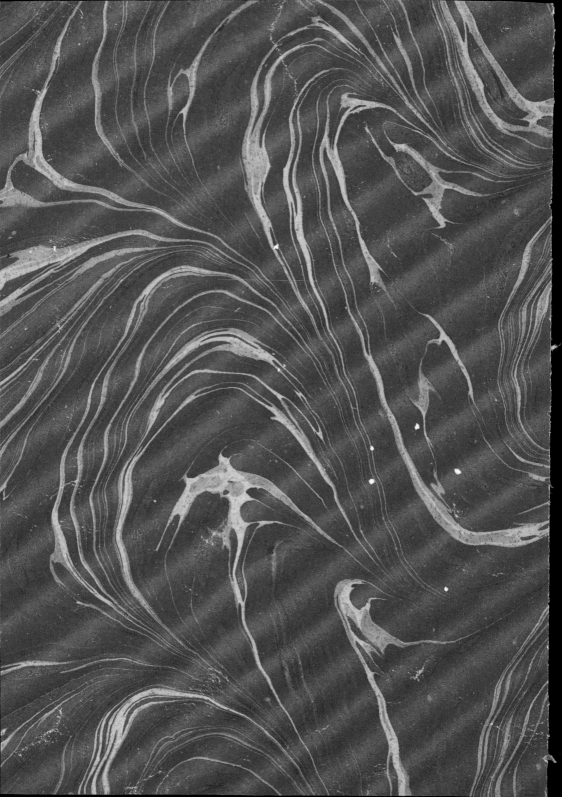